That's Not Fair!

That's Not Fair!

Why Do Good Things Happen to Bad People?

Galal Ahmed

WITH Angie Ahmed
ON CHAPTERS 2 AND 4

RESOURCE *Publications* · Eugene, Oregon

THAT'S NOT FAIR!
Why Do Good Things Happen to Bad People?

Resource Publications
An Imprint of Wipf and Stock Publishers
199 W. 8th Ave., Suite 3
Eugene, OR 97401

www.wipfandstock.com

PAPERBACK ISBN: 979-8-3852-5793-5
HARDCOVER ISBN: 979-8-3852-5794-2
EBOOK ISBN: 979-8-3852-5795-9

VERSION NUMBER 08/15/25

This book is dedicated to my children, Tulip Sameha, London Comfort and Judah Washer. Your Baba is a great sinner but never forget that Christ is a great Savior! He is the treasure hidden in a field, He is the pearl of great price, He is the bronze serpent lifted up on a pole! Look to Him and live! "The father of the righteous will greatly rejoice, and he who begets a wise child will delight in him. Let your father and your mother be glad, and let her who bore you rejoice." Proverbs 23:24, 25 NKJV

Contents

Preface

THERE IS A WELL-KNOWN story in Islam that is narrated in the Hadiths about a man who killed 99 persons. This is the version of it from Sahih al-Bukhari: "The Prophet said, 'Amongst the men of Bani Israel there was a man who had murdered 99 persons. Then he set out asking (whether his repentance could be accepted or not). He came upon a monk and asked him if his repentance could be accepted. The monk replied in the negative and so the man killed him. He kept on asking till a man advised to go to such and such village. (So he left for it) but death overtook him on the way. While dying, he turned his chest towards that village (where he had hoped his repentance would be accepted), and so the angels of mercy and the angels of punishment quarreled amongst themselves regarding him. Allah ordered the village (towards which he was going) to come closer to him, and ordered the village (whence he had come), to go far away, and then He ordered the angels to measure the distances between his body and the two villages. So he was found to be one span closer to the village (he was going to). So he was forgiven.'"[1] Among Muslims, this is a wonderful story about Allah's great mercy and forgiveness. I was raised by a Muslim father and have heard this story recited many times. Later on, we shall see why this story is not so wonderful at all.

While living in Norfolk, Virginia, I worked as a roofer for 6 years, giving people estimates for new roofs or repairs. Every day I would have around 5 or 6 appointments with a 2-hour window for each one. A typical day would consist of driving to people's homes all over the Hampton Roads area, walking their roofs, going in attics to try and find leaks, etc. If they needed a

---

1. *Sahih al-Bukhari*, trans. Muhammad Muhsin Khan, vol. 4, Book 56, Hadith 676 (Riyadh: Darussalam, 1997).

repair, I would end up doing it myself, but if a new roof was needed, the crew would come out another day for that task. My boss was a Christian and saw his business as a ministry. He encouraged me to share the gospel with the customers as I had the opportunity. Every time I would give a customer an estimate, I would always include a gospel tract in the folder with the paperwork. I loved my job because, having a passion for the lost, I was able to have many conversations with them about the gospel. It was incredible! I would like to share one of those encounters with you.

Monday morning had arrived. The weekend was over, and it was time for work again. I woke up early so I could go for a run, take a quick shower, and get dressed for the day. Afterwards, I read and prayed, asking God for help in sharing the gospel with my customers today. I prayed for wisdom, love, and boldness. He *always* answers that prayer. I headed out the front door and checked my truck's toolbox along with the 24-foot ladder on top. I made sure my tools were packed, my paperwork was ready, and the ladder was locked down tight with those straps. The last thing I needed was for my ladder to go flying off my truck while I was going 65 mph on the highway! I then got in the front seat and started heading to my first appointment.

I pulled up to this house not too far from Old Dominion University (ODU) and got out of my truck. I walked up to the front door and gave it a knock. As the customer opened the door, I introduced myself, "Hello, my name is Galal Ahmed from J. Montes Roofing. I am here to give you an estimate for a roof replacement."

The man who answered the door was Middle Eastern-looking and was also a student at ODU. I asked him to give me a few minutes so I could take some measurements and write up an estimate for a new roof. About 20 minutes later, I went back up to his front door with the estimate in hand. He came outside, and I went over the estimate with him.

As I did, I noticed he had a Muslim name, so I asked him about his name, "Are you a Muslim? I ask because you have an Islamic name." Most Muslims I meet will either have Ahmed or Muhammed in their name. He told me he was a Muslim and went to the mosque that was located on the campus of ODU. I have been there before with my dad, so I was familiar with it. I told him that my father is also a Muslim. I shared with him how my dad is from Cairo, Egypt, and how my whole family on my dad's side are all Muslims. They all live in Egypt, Saudi Arabia, and Kuwait.

We chatted briefly about our backgrounds and religious upbringings. I then asked him this question, "So as a Muslim, what do you think happens when we die?"

He said, "Well, it depends how you live your life. If you are a good Muslim, then you will go to paradise. If you are not, then you will end up in the hellfire."

I said, "Where are you going to end up? Are you a good Muslim?"

He said, "I try to be."

I said, "Well, let's find out. I am going to ask you some of the 10 Commandments to see how you will do on Judgement Day. Can you handle that?"

He said, "Sure."

Muslims believe Moses was a prophet who God gave the 10 Commandments too. They also believe Jesus was a prophet. So, with that in mind, I said, "The 9th Commandment says, 'Thou shalt not lie.' How many lies have you told?"[2]

"Several," was his answer.

I asked, "What do you call someone who has told several lies?"

He said, "A liar."

I said, "Have you ever stolen anything? That is the 8th Commandment."[3]

He said, "No."

I responded with, "Are you sure? You have never downloaded music illegally or cheated on a test, which is stealing answers?"

He laughed and said, "Okay, I have done that."

I said, "So what do you call someone who has stolen?"

He said, "A thief."

I asked him, "Have you ever taken God's name in vain?"

He said, "I have."

I said, "That is called blasphemy. The Bible says, 'The LORD will not hold him guiltless who takes His name in vain.'"[4] One to go. Jesus, the Prophet, said, 'Whoever looks at a woman to lust for her has already committed adultery with her in his heart.' Have you done that?"[5]

He got a big smile on his face and said, "I have."

---

2. Exodus 20:16 (New King James Version).

3. Exodus 20:15 (New King James Version).

4. Exodus 20:7 (New King James Version).

5. Matthew 5:28 (New King James Version).

I then said, "I am not judging you, but by your own admission, you are a lying thief, a blasphemer, and an adulterer at heart. Would you be innocent or guilty for breaking God's Law?"

He said, "Guilty."

I said, "Heaven or hell?"

He said, "If I repent, I will go to heaven."

I said, "Try that in court. Hey Judge, I shot the guard, robbed the bank, but I am really sorry for doing that and will never do it again. Would that Judge let him go?"

He laughed and said, "No."

I said, "Of course not. God's court is far higher than man's court. If that won't work in man's courts, it definitely won't work in God's. God is holy, righteous, just, and good. So, your repentance can't save you. And any so-called 'good works' are mere attempts to bribe God, which will actually make your punishment far worse."

I continued, "So according to the Bible, you would end up in hell. Revelation 21:8 says, '...All *liars* will have their part in the lake of fire.' 1 Corinthians 6:9-10 says, 'Do you not know that the unrighteous will not inherit the kingdom of God? Do not be deceived. Neither fornicators, nor idolaters, nor *adulterers*, nor homosexuals, nor sodomites, nor *thieves*, nor covetous, nor drunkards, nor revilers, nor extortioners will inherit the kingdom of God.'[6] You are in big trouble, my friend. Do you see that?"

He nodded his head yes. I was excited at this point. The Law had stopped his mouth and showed him that he was guilty before a holy God. I said, "Let's go back to the court analogy for a second. Let's say you broke a bunch of laws, and now you owe a fine of $1,000,000 dollars. If you can't pay the fine, you are going to jail for the rest of your life. But just before the Judge passes sentence, someone steps into the courtroom on your behalf and pays your fine. All of it! The Judge says, 'The fine has been paid, you are free to go.' How would that make you feel?"

He said, "Happy and grateful."

I said, "Exactly! That, my friend, is what Jesus did for sinners 2,000 years ago. Sinners broke God's Law, the 10 Commandments, and Jesus paid the fine. That is what the cross is all about. Christ lived a perfect life, suffered and died on the cross, taking the wrath of God for sin, and rose from the dead 3 days later. He did that for every person who would ever believe in Him. That is the only way you can be right with God. You must repent

6. Revelation 21:8; 1 Corinthians 6:9–10 (New King James Version).

and trust in Christ alone. The moment you do that, God will forgive you for ALL of your sins, past, present, and future, not because you are good, but because He is good and kind and rich in mercy."

The young man's response was priceless. He said, "*THAT'S NOT FAIR! It is not fair for someone else to take the punishment you deserve.*"

I said, "You are right, my friend. That's *not* fair. That is *GRACE!* Do you remember the story in the Hadiths about the man who killed 99 people?"

He said, "I do."

I said, "So after the man killed 100 people, he died on his way to the village where his repentance would be accepted. Remember what happened next?"

He nodded in agreement.

I said, "The two angels fought over his body, and Allah shrunk the earth so that the man would be closer to the good village, and his repentance would be accepted, and he would be forgiven."[7]

I then asked him, "Is *that* fair?"

He smiled and said, "No."

I said, "Exactly! That is not fair. *That* is actually evil. That is like a judge who has someone standing before him who slaughtered an entire family. He tells the judge he is sorry, and he won't do it again. The Judge smiles and says, that's okay, I am merciful and forgiving. You are free to go. If a judge did that, he would be *more* evil than the man who committed all those murders in the first place."

His eyes got really big, like the size of Emeal Zwayne's from Living Waters.

I then explained to him that this is *the* difference between Islam and Christianity. In Islam, when Allah forgives people, he is not just. But in Christianity, when God forgives His people, He is not only just, but the justifier of those who have faith in Jesus! The keeping of God's Law and the punishment for breaking His Law are accomplished and satisfied perfectly in the life and death of Jesus Christ. This is what we call the active and passive obedience of Christ.

"But now the righteousness of God apart from the law is revealed, being witnessed by the Law and the Prophets, even the righteousness of God, through faith in Jesus Christ, to all and on all who believe. For there is no difference; for all have sinned and fall short of the glory of God, being justified freely by His grace through the redemption that is in Christ

7. *Sahih al-Bukhari*, trans. Muhammad Muhsin Khan, vol. 4, Book 56, Hadith 676.

Jesus, whom God set forth as a propitiation by His blood, through faith, to demonstrate His righteousness, because in His forbearance God had passed over the sins that were previously committed, to demonstrate at the present time His righteousness, that He might be *just* and the justifier of the one who has faith in Jesus."[8]

I gave him some Christian literature and pleaded with him to please think about this. I told him to transfer his trust from himself, which is self-righteousness, to the *only* Savior, Jesus Christ. He thanked me for the conversation and said he enjoyed it very much. It gave him lots to think about. We parted ways, and I was off to my next appointment. I prayed for him and thanked God for being able to share the gospel with him. I hope to see that man in heaven one day.

This is why I titled the book, "That's Not Fair!" All we deserve is God's wrath. Everything else is grace. I want to share with you my testimony, which is not fair, my wife's, which isn't fair either, and many others in history and throughout the Bible, whose testimonies are not fair. They are stories of God's amazing *grace*! I also want to give some other aspects of why good things happen to bad people, such as my being a husband, a father, and an evangelist. My prayer and hope are for God's glorious nature and character to be magnified throughout this book. As John the Baptist once said, "He must increase, and I must decrease."[9] That is what this book is all about. It is about God's perfections being put on display through the lives of fallen men and women. "For of Him and through Him and to Him are all things, to whom be glory forever. Amen."[10] Soli Deo Gloria!

Doxology
Written by Thomas Ken, 1674

Praise God, from whom all blessings flow;
Praise Him, all creatures here below;
Praise Him above, ye heav'nly host;
Praise Father, Son, and Holy Ghost. Amen.[11]

---

8. Romans 3:21–26 (New King James Version)

9. John 3:30 (New King James Version).

10. Romans 11:36 (New King James Version).

11. Thomas Ken, "Doxology," in *Manual of Prayers for the Use of the Scholars of Winchester College* (London: n.p., 1674).

Chapter 1

Part 1

A Brand Plucked from the Fire

"If you can sin and not weep over it, you are an heir of Hell. If you can go into sin, and afterwards feel satisfied to have done so, you are on the road to destruction. If there are no prickings of conscience, no inward torments, no bleeding wounds; if you have no throbs and heavings of a bosom that cannot rest; if your soul never feels filled with wormwood and gall when you know you have done evil, you are no child of God." Charles Spurgeon[1]

WHY DO GOOD THINGS happen to bad people? This is THE question to be asked. My testimony is an answer to this question which gives glory to the True and Living God. My name is Galal Maher Ahmed. I was born in Stillwater, Oklahoma, June 1st, 1982, the same year Buc-ee's was founded. Coincidence? I think not. That is called providence! (I really like Buc-ee's. Their pulled pork sandwiches are the best.) My father is from Cairo, Egypt, and is a Muslim. My mother is from Browning, Montana, and is a Christian (NOW). So, that makes me half Egyptian. Or as I like to say, half terrorist.

---

1. Charles H. Spurgeon, "A Jealous God," in The New Park Street Pulpit Sermons, vol. 6 (London: Passmore & Alabaster, 1860), 121

I was not raised in a Christian home. I was taken to the Mosque after Ramadan during their feast (Eid al-Fitr) when I was very young with my dad and went to Church on Sundays up through high school with my mom, reluctantly. The whole idea of God, Church, and the Bible bored me to death. I used to pretend to be sick to avoid going to Church. If that didn't work, I would fall asleep during the worship service. My mom would get so angry she would tell me, "Go sleep in the car!"

A Youth Marked by Sin

Growing up, I was a shy kid. I would get embarrassed easily and was very quiet. In school, I would often get bullied and picked on for my name or my coarse hair (back when I had some) or whatever else. Kids don't need a reason to pick on you. They are just plain mean. After being bullied so much, I started to work out and lift weights. I figured if I got bigger, they might not mess with me as much, and I would be able to defend myself physically. Exercise helped me physically, but it also stirred up my narcissistic tendencies. I had a great fear of man. Instead of being afraid of getting made fun of, now I was getting their praises and wanted more. Both were rooted in fear of man. I also found some old VHS tapes with pornographic movies on them while I was in 5th grade. Those wicked images awakened my flesh to lust that I never knew of and wished I never had. From that point on in my life, the lust in my heart grew greater and greater. I also had a very bad temper growing up. I fought a lot in middle school and high school. Some kids would call me the "White Mike Tyson."

Chasing Signs and Wonders

I made many professions of faith throughout my high school years. The church I went to was an Assemblies of God. I "asked Jesus into my heart" at least 15 times or so and raised my hand and walked the aisle about half a dozen times. The message I remember hearing was a life enhancement message with supernatural experiences emphasized. It was about some person taking a trip to heaven or Jesus appearing to someone in their bedroom, etc. It was all about signs and wonders. The whole church would be praying together, and then the congregation would break out into "tongues" all at once, which sounded pretty wild. It was quite entertaining for a teenager. There were over a thousand people in the church, so you can imagine how noisy it was. The "Christianity" I was exposed to was all about health and wealth mixed in with some supernatural experiences. It was another gospel which was no gospel at all, see Galatians 1:6-7.[2] I called myself a Christian and was a defender of people like Benny Hinn and Jesse Duplantis, both of whom are heretics. I read a book my mom bought for me back when I was in high school called Good Morning, Holy Spirit by Benny Hinn.[3] I hated to read back then and refused to read anything. I wouldn't even read cliff notes for school, but for some reason, I read that book. I also watched a video called Close Encounters of the God Kind by Jesse Duplantis.[4] Those two resources shaped my understanding of what I believed Christianity was all about.

Life Adrift in the Navy

I joined the Navy right after I graduated high school in August of 2000. I did 2½ months at boot camp in Great Lakes, IL. When I completed boot camp, I got stationed in Norfolk, VA, on the USS Trenton. I was an undesignated seaman assigned to the USS Trenton, which is an amphibious ship. After being in the Navy for a year, I was able to go back to Great Lakes, IL, for A-school. While I was in A-school, I took a physical test to see if I would get accepted for the Navy Dive School. I passed the test, so I got stationed back in Norfolk, VA, as a "mud pup". We were the cool guys who wore super short tan shorts with a white t-shirt as we trained every day. We would go for 6-mile runs and do pushups and pull-ups until failure. We also had 2 pool days a week. I had about 6 months in Virginia until my Dive School class began in Pensacola, FL.

While I was stationed in Virginia, I met my first wife at church. She was 16, and I was 19. It was a Baptist church, and I remember arguing with folks there about tongues, healings, and trips to heaven. I was ignorant of the Bible, so I would just say whatever Benny Hinn or Jesse Duplantis would preach and teach. We ended up going to a different church after we started dating because I was charismatic. I wanted to go to a church that practiced "tongues, healings, and supernatural experiences." So, we started going to

2. Galatians 1:6-7 (New King James Version).

3. Benny Hinn, Good Morning, Holy Spirit (Nashville: Thomas Nelson, 1990).

4. Jesse Duplantis, Close Encounters of the God Kind (Metairie, LA: Jesse Duplantis Ministries, 1996), DVD.

Greenbriar Church in Chesapeake. This church actually had a class teaching people how to speak in tongues. Chapter and verse please?

On Memorial Day weekend, I went home to visit my family and friends. While I was out with my friends from high school, we did what we normally did for fun back then. We went egging. We first had to go to the grocery store and buy a few dozen eggs. Eggs were cheap back then. My buddy Watson had a white Camaro with T-tops. It was pretty nice. So I rode shotgun, and Bobby was in the backseat. As Watson drove us around, we threw eggs as we drove by cars going the opposite direction of us. After throwing egg after egg and watching the car's brake lights come on, which made us laugh so hard, we were down to our last egg. It was about midnight and dark outside. You couldn't make out the other cars too well. Then I called dibs on throwing the last egg. We saw a car coming toward us from a distance. I got ready with the egg and launched it out of the top of the car through the T-tops perfectly. It hit the car driving by us right in the middle of the windshield. The car's brake lights came on, and so did the red and blue lights on top of it. It was a police car! I didn't realize that when I threw the egg until it was too late. The cop turned around with a vengeance and pulled us over.

Long story short, I got arrested. I was charged with a misdemeanor, throwing an object at a moving vehicle. I pleaded guilty. My grandma ended up bailing me out of jail the next day after my flight had already left. So, I was absent without authorization (UA) for a couple of days, and that eventually led to them kicking me out of the Dive program. I was pretty upset, but there was no one to blame but myself. I really wanted to be a Navy Diver.

I got reassigned to a Destroyer in San Diego, California. My first wife and I had a long-distance relationship until I got out in 2004. During that time, my lust kept growing and growing. I remember saying to myself that this whole lust thing would get better in time. I would say, "Once I get engaged, I will stop looking at porn." Didn't happen. Then I would say, "Once I get married, I will quit." Didn't happen. I was a slave to sin.

After I got out of the military, in August of 2004, I moved back to Virginia. I got hired on with the Fire Department about a year later. One of the best jobs in the world. I got married at the same time. During that time, I was still a professing Christian. I just never read my Bible or prayed, unless I was in church or wanted something. Church was a place to have community. I loved watching TBN, Trinity Broadcasting

Network, that was my channel. I would watch people there who would teach on prophecy or talk about some experience they had on a supposed trip to heaven, or even hell.

Confronted by the Law

Early in the year 2006, I came across a show on TBN called The Way of the Master. It was like nothing I had ever seen before. These guys would go out on the street and talk with strangers about the things of God. It was the most fascinating thing that I had ever seen. The two men hosting it and doing the interviews were Ray Comfort and Kirk Cameron.[5] I would watch their show and think to myself, "What they are saying is very different than what I hear other preachers saying on the *same* station!" They would ask people what they think happens after they die. Then they would ask them if they think they are a good person. Almost everyone would say that they were (Proverbs 20:6).[6] Next, they would ask them if they have kept the Ten Commandments and how would they do on Judgment Day. Finally, they would share the message of the gospel as they called people to repentance and faith in Christ.

In August of 2006, I was watching their show, and as they asked people questions, I asked myself the same ones. Of course, I believed I was a good person. I mean, come on, I was a Veteran with an honorable discharge. I was also a Norfolk firefighter. I was a hero! I would risk my life to save others! I also rode the ambulance and would start IVs on people and take them to the ER or work on them at the scene. If anyone could claim to be a good person, it was me, right? Wrong!

I came face to face with God's Law. It was like a mirror that showed me what I am in truth (James 1:23-25; 2:11-12).[7] The first question came, "How many lies have you told?"

"Lots."

"What do you call someone who has told many lies?" A liar.

"Have you ever stolen anything?" Yep. I stole a lot as a teenager at the mall just for fun with my friends.

"What do you call someone who steals things?" A thief.

---

5. Ray Comfort and Kirk Cameron, The Way of the Master, television program (Santa Clarita, CA: Living Waters Publications, 2003–present).

6. Proverbs 20:6 (New King James Version).

7. James 1:23-25; 2:11-12 (New King James Version).

"Have you ever taken God's name in vain?"

Yes.

"That is called blasphemy, and the Bible says, 'The LORD will not hold him guiltless who takes His name in vain.'"[8]

Then the fatal blow came. "Jesus said that whoever looks at a woman with lust HAS committed adultery with her in his heart. Have you ever done that?"[9] All the time! I was guilty.

As a firefighter, I would work 10 days a month and have the other 20 off. I would come home from work and get on the laptop and look at porn after my first wife went to work. I would get in chat rooms looking for girls to exchange dirty pics and have sexual conversations with. I remember feeling real Holy Spirit-wrought conviction of sin in that moment. Suddenly, I realized I was NOT a good person. I was a sinful, wicked, vile wretch, like the Bible says I am. I was doubly guilty of self-righteousness as well, because I said I was a good person when I was not. The Law shut my mouth and left me condemned where I stood (Romans 3:19-20).[10]

In that moment, I saw that I was naked and exposed before a holy, righteous God (Hebrews 4:12-13).[11] I was a false convert. I would have been the man from Matthew 7:21-23 who cried out to the Lord on Judgment Day saying, "Lord, Lord," and He would have said to me, "Depart from Me, you who practice lawlessness."[12] 1 John 1:6 pierced my soul with conviction, which says, "If we say that we have fellowship with Him, and walk in darkness, we lie and do not practice the truth."[13] That was me, a liar. I claimed to be a Christian, but I really walked in darkness and LOVED it. I was "wretched, miserable, poor, blind, and naked" (Revelation 3:17).[14] I realized what I truly deserved: hell. It would have been my just desserts. Any excuse or objection I could have raised was futile.

In the video, some of the people would still try to object. They would say, "Well, what about all the 'good' I have done?"

Ray's response: "Try that in court. Judge, I robbed the bank and shot the guard. But I have done a lot of good deeds." That is not how courts work.

8. Exodus 20:7 (New King James Version).

9. Matthew 5:28 (New King James Version).

10. Romans 3:19-20 (New King James Version).

11. Hebrews 4:12-13 (New King James Version).

12. Matthew 7:21-23 (New King James Version).

13. 1 John 1:6 (New King James Version).

14. Revelation 3:17 (New King James Version).

You are not judged for what you did right but for what you did wrong. Good judges punish lawbreakers. That is justice. God is the Just Judge who ALWAYS does that which is right (Genesis 18:25).[15]

Some would try to minimize their sin and say, "But my sins are not that bad." I mean, I have never killed anyone or raped anyone before. Think of it like this. Let's take lying, for example. Let's say you lie to your dog. What is going to happen to you? Nothing. It's a dog. Let's say you lie to your wife. You might be sleeping on the couch. Let's say you lie to your boss. You could lose your job. Let's say you are in court under oath, and you lie. You could go to jail for a couple of years for perjury. What has changed in each scenario? Why is the punishment greater in some instances than in others? What has changed is the authority of the one whom the crime was committed against. Little authority, little punishment. Great authority, great punishment. All sin is against an INFINITE, HOLY, RIGHTEOUS GOD (Psalm 51:4).[16] Therefore, the punishment is in direct proportion to who HE is. That is why Hell is FOREVER. Eternal Conscious Torment. It is not the greatness of the sin that is the issue. The issue is the thrice-holy God whom that sin is committed against. THAT is the issue.

Think about this for a minute, how many sins did Adam commit in the garden? One. He ate from the tree that God forbade him to. That might sound petty to you and me. I mean, come on, he just ate a piece of fruit. Cut him some slack. Give him a break. No, my friend. As R.C. Sproul once said, "This creature from the dirt defied the everlasting, holy God!"[17] Because of that one transgression, God cursed the entire Earth (Genesis 3:17-19)![18] That is how serious our sin is to a HOLY God. That is why God says in His Word, "All liars will have their place in the lake of fire. And no thief, blasphemer, or adulterer will inherit the kingdom of God (Revelation 21:8; 1 Corinthians 6:9-10)."[19] It's because God is GOOD! He ALONE is good (Mark 10:18).[20]

15. Genesis 18:25 (New King James Version

16. Psalm 51:4 (New King James Version).

17. R.C. Sproul, "The Curse Motif of the Atonement," lecture delivered at Ligonier Ministries National Conference, Orlando, FL, 2008.

18. Genesis 3:17-19 (New King James Version).

19. Revelation 21:8; 1 Corinthians 6:9-10 (New King James Version).

20. Mark 10:18 (New King James Version).

God is a consuming fire (Hebrews 12:29)![21] What a fearful thing it is to fall into the hands of the living God (Hebrews 10:31)![22]

The Glorious Gospel

After seeing I was condemned by the Law, I heard the most glorious Gospel EVER! "But God, who is rich in MERCY, because of His great love with which He loved us, even when we were dead in trespasses, made us alive together with Christ (by grace you have been saved), and raised us up to-gether, and made us sit together in the heavenly places in Christ Jesus, that in the ages to come He might show the exceeding riches of His grace in His kindness toward us in Christ Jesus" (Ephesians 2:4-7).[23]

Imagine you broke the law and had to go before a Judge. As you stand before him, you are told that you owe one million dollars in fines for all the laws you have broken. You now have one of two options. Either you pay your fine, or you spend the rest of your life in prison with no parole. So, you say, "Well, I can't pay that, so I guess I have no other option but to go to prison."

Suddenly, the Judge Himself says, "I am going to pay your fine in FULL. Your fine has been paid, and you are FREE to go!"

How would you feel towards that Judge? Thankful! Grateful!

Well, here is the Good News of the Gospel! God the Judge became a Man in the person of Jesus Christ. The Second Person of the Trinity took on flesh! Jesus is truly God and truly Man! He kept the Law that you and I have broken our entire lives. He NEVER sinned once! He always did that which pleased the Father. He fulfilled all righteousness. Then He went to the cross willingly. On that cross, He bore our sins as He suffered and died. He took the wrath of God that we deserved in FULL! Then He rose from the dead three days later, defeating death! Forty days later, He ascended to heaven and is now seated at the right hand of the Father, where He now rules and reigns as well as intercedes for His people! We broke God's Law, the Ten Commandments, and Jesus paid the fine in full! That is why Jesus cried out on the cross TETELESTAI before He died, which means, PAID IN FULL (John 19:30)!

---

21. Hebrews 12:29 (New King James Version).

22. Hebrews 10:31 (New King James Version

23. Ephesians 2:4-7 (New King James Version).

God is not only just but He is the justifier of those who have faith in His Son! That is the best news EVER! This is THE great exchange! Christ took His people's sins (past, present, and future) on Himself as He was crushed by the Father's wrath. In exchange, He gives us His perfect righteousness as a gift! To be right with God and enjoy Him forever in Heaven, we need not only to be forgiven of our sins, which brings us to neutrality, but we need to have perfect righteousness. Jesus Himself said that we must be perfect, just as the Father in heaven is perfect. That is what He has done for me! I have the perfect righteousness of Jesus Christ! 2 Corinthians 5:21 says, "He made Him who knew no sin to be sin for us, so that we might become the righteousness of God in Him."[24]

How did I receive this free gift? Through repentance and faith in Christ ALONE! Repentance and faith are gifts from God! By God's amazing grace, I turned from my sin and placed my trust in Christ alone. Think of it like this. You are on a plane about to jump ten thousand feet. Someone asks you what you are going to do. You say, "I am going to flap my arms really, really hard."

"Yikes! Don't do that," the man says. "Put on the parachute! Put your trust in IT!"

That is what the Bible tells sinners to do in Romans 13:14, "But put on the Lord Jesus Christ, and make no provision for the flesh, to fulfill its lusts."[25] Do NOT trust in yourself. Put your trust fully in Christ ALONE!

A Wretch Redeemed

Not only does God justify the ungodly (Romans 4:5),[26] but He adopts them as sons and daughters (Galatians 4:5).[27] For the believer, He is no longer Judge but now their Father. I was born again in October of 2006. I was dead at the bottom of a horrible pit, and God graciously brought me up out of that horrible pit, out of the miry clay, and set my feet upon a rock (Psalm 40:2).[28] That Rock was and is Christ! So that is the beginning of my story. I was 24 years old when God graciously saved a wretch like me!

24. 2 Corinthians 5:21 (New King James Version
25. Romans 13:14 (New King James Version).
26. Romans 4:5 (New King James Version).
27. Galatians 4:5 (New King James Version).
28. Psalm 40:2 (New King James Version).

Amazing Grace
Written by John Newton, 1779

Amazing grace! (how sweet the sound)
That sav'd a wretch like me!
I once was lost, but now am found,
Was blind, but now I see.

'Twas grace that taught my heart to fear,
And grace my fears reliev'd;
How precious did that grace appear,
The hour I first believ'd!

Thro' many dangers, toils and snares,
I have already come;
'Tis grace has brought me safe thus far,
And grace will lead me home.[29]

29. John Newton, "Amazing Grace," in Olney Hymns (London: W. Oliver, 1779), no. 41

Part 2

A Man After David's Own Heart

"So David said to Nathan, 'I have sinned against the LORD.' And Nathan said to David, 'The LORD also has put away your sin; you shall not die. However, because by this deed you have given great occasion to the enemies of the LORD to blaspheme, the child also who is born to you shall surely die.'"[1]

Newton's 3rd Law

I WISH I COULD give you a different experience I had from this point forward, but that would just not be true. Amid God's amazing hand of providence as He reached down into my wicked heart and gave me a new one, there remained indwelling sin as well as consequences for my sins before I was converted. George Whitefield once said, "After we are renewed, yet we are renewed but in part, indwelling sin continues in us, there is a mixture of corruption in every one of our duties; so that after we are converted, were Jesus Christ only to accept us according to our works, our works would damn us, for we cannot put up a prayer but it is far from that perfection which the moral Law requireth. I do not know what you may think, but I can say that I cannot pray but I sin—I cannot preach to you or

---

1. 2 Samuel 12:13-14 (New King James Version).

others but I sin—I can do nothing without sin; and, as one expresseth it, my repentance wants to be repented of, and my tears to be washed in the precious blood of my dear Redeemer."[2]

God saved me in October of 2006. Two months BEFORE that, in August, I was on my laptop while my first wife was at work. As usual, I was looking at pornography and talking to other girls in chat rooms, sending pics, and having sexual conversations. In this instance, I ended up talking to a minor online. We had a brief conversation that was sexual in nature. I also sent dirty pictures to her. We talked for about 15-20 minutes in the chat room. After that, we never spoke again. I never tried to meet her or ever intended on it. I sinned very wickedly against God and her that day.

Fast forward to February 1st, 2007, 6 months later, I am home from work and get a knock on my front door. It is the police. They come rushing inside to arrest me and search my house. Come to find out, the girl I spoke with online 6 months ago was not a real girl. It was an undercover cop posing as a minor. I was charged with two class 6 felonies: Use of communications to solicit a minor for sex and indecent liberties with a minor attempt. I got released from jail on a PR bond the next day. Then my Fire Chief and Captain showed up at my house and told me I was terminated from the Fire Department. The day after that, the news reporters stopped by my house wanting to do an interview with me about the crime I committed. I have never experienced such shame and humiliation like that in my life. I went from being one of the most beloved people, a firefighter, to one of the most despised people, a sex offender.

Shame and Loss

My final court hearing was in October of 2007. I was given a total of 10 years to serve with 9 years and 9 months suspended. So, I had to do 3 months in jail along with a 7-year probation period after getting out. If I violated my probation during those 7 years, they could give me back the other 9 years and 9 months. At this point, my first wife was very supportive of me. But after being in jail for those 3 months, she had a change of heart. The day I got out, January 20th, 2008, she told me she no longer loved me and wanted a divorce. Our marriage lasted just shy of 2 years.

---

2. George Whitefield, "The Method of Grace," in Select Sermons of George Whitefield (London: Banner of Truth Trust, 1958), 75–76.

The War Within

After getting out, I reported to my probation officer (PO) and was not ready for what awaited me. I had LOTS of restrictions. I had a 10pm curfew, was not allowed to live within so many feet of a school, had no access to the internet, was not allowed to live with any minors or even be around them, had to do 2 years of sex offender treatment and take polygraphs, etc. To say there were consequences would be an understatement. The hardest part about this whole situation was my sin. It didn't just go away as much as I wanted it to. The big change was instead of LOVING my sin, I now HATED it. The war inside me began. John Owen once said, "Be killing sin, or sin will be killing you."[3]

Hope in the Gospels

One thing that was so encouraging to me and still is, was this: As I read through the Gospels, I noticed how Jesus treated sinners; the outcast, the despised, and the filthy of the world. He had compassion for them, and it encouraged me greatly! He loved them to the utmost! Pick your sinner, and you see Christ love them like no one else did. Whether it was Matthew the Tax Collector, the sinful woman at the Pharisee's house, or the Prodigal Son, He showed them compassion. Christ not only treated them with compassion but died for them, SHOWING them He really loved them. Romans 5:8 says, "But God demonstrates His own love toward us, in that while we were still sinners, Christ died for us."[4]

My favorite passage in the whole Bible is Matthew 11:28-30. In it, Jesus says, "Come to Me, all you who labor and are heavy laden, and I will give you rest. Take My yoke upon you and learn from Me, for I am gentle and lowly in heart, and you will find rest for your souls. For My yoke is easy and My burden is light."[5]

Praise God! I was a new creature in Christ. I read and devoured His Word. I loved gathering with His people every Sunday to worship Him. I prayed and prayed because I was so weak. I was like a sponge when it came to the things of God. I now, as a real Christian, loved God and loved

3. John Owen, The Mortification of Sin (1656; repr., Edinburgh: Banner of Truth Trust, 2004), 47

4. Romans 5:8 (New King James Version).

5. Matthew 11:28-30 (New King James Version).

people. Ray Comfort was my mentor from afar and still is. I also found other wonderful preachers such as Paul Washer, John MacArthur, Voddie Baucham, and Todd Friel. God was so kind to me through this all. I would share the gospel with anyone I could. I had a lot of zeal with very little knowledge. I have heard it once said of D.L. Moody that he was known for having "zeal without knowledge." I was in good company. Being a child of God, I experienced His love, mercy, and grace, which still overwhelms me. My sin is GREAT, but my Savior is GREATER! Where sin abounds, grace abounds that much more! I have such a love and zeal for the Lord because of how much I have been forgiven.

Jesus said, "She loved much because she had been forgiven much."[6] That is ME! I have been reading the Bible now for 19 years since God saved me, and I think I may have finally found a mistake.

In 1 Timothy 1:15, Paul says, "This is a faithful saying and worthy of all acceptance, that Christ Jesus came into the world to save sinners, of whom I am chief."[7] Sorry Paul, you are not the chief of sinners anymore, I am!

Depression and Despair

The next 5 years were very hard and lonely. Finding a job was nearly impossible, being a registered sex offender and a convicted felon. I also continued to struggle with sexual sin, *a lot*. I never truly understood what it meant to be depressed. Now I did. In March of 2012, God, the Holy Spirit, convicted me of looking at porn and meeting girls from online dating sites. I repented to the Lord and met with a friend from church to confess my sins. As we talked, he told me I needed to tell my PO. The thought of that terrified me because I knew what could happen. I could go back to jail. But I was truly repentant and had godly sorrow for what I had done and wanted to make things right.

"For observe this very thing, that you sorrowed in a godly manner: What diligence it produced in you, what clearing of yourselves, what indignation, what fear, what vehement desire, what zeal, what vindication! In all things you proved yourselves to be clear in this matter" (2 Corinthians 7:11).[8] I was supposed to see my PO the following week for a monthly

6. Luke 7:47 (New King James Version).

7. 1 Timothy 1:15 (New King James Version).

8. 2 Corinthians 7:11 (New King James Version).

check-up. I told her about what I have been doing and told her I was sorry for sinning. I was ready to accept whatever consequences I had coming. She surprisingly did not punish me. She showed me mercy, and I did not have to go back to jail.

Not long after that, I got to such a low point in my life where I didn't want to live anymore. I was seriously contemplating suicide. I began to look up ways to kill myself. So, after being on probation for 5 years, I stopped caring about my restrictions. I bought myself a smartphone, which was a violation of my probation, and kept it hidden from my PO. On my monthly visit to see her in December of 2012, I was caught with my smartphone. It was a violation of my probation, so I got sent back to jail. I did 6 months this time. When I got released in May 2013, I was given 7 years of probation, AGAIN. I also had to do 2 more years of treatment with polygraphs, AGAIN.

God's Unfailing Grace

Through all this, God continued to love me and pour out His grace upon me. My story is a story of God's patience with His children. It is a story about a Father who pursues and disciplines His child in love. He will NEVER let me go.

"And I give them eternal life, and they shall never perish; neither shall anyone snatch them out of My hand. My Father, who has given them to Me, is greater than all; and no one is able to snatch them out of My Father's hand. I and My Father are one" (John 10:28-30).[9] He is sovereign over EVERYTHING, even my sin. So why do good things happen to bad people? Because of God's amazing GRACE! Grace stands for "God's riches at Christ's Expense." Grace is unmerited favor to hell-deserving sinners. That is WHY! God loves to save sinners, especially the WORST of sinners like me.

The Only Appropriate Response

So, in light of all that, a passage comes to mind where God met Moses on Mount Sinai. When God went before him, this is what He proclaimed to Moses about Himself: "The LORD, the LORD God, merciful and

9. John 10:28-30 (New King James Version).

GRACIOUS, longsuffering, and abounding in goodness and truth, keeping mercy for thousands, forgiving iniquity and transgression and sin, by no means clearing the guilty, visiting the iniquity of the fathers upon the children and the children's children to the third and the fourth generation" (Exodus 34:6-7).[10] The ONLY appropriate response is what Moses did in the next verse: "So Moses made haste and bowed his head toward the earth, and WORSHIPED."[11] Let us do likewise!

10. Exodus 34:6-7 (New King James Version

11. Exodus 34:8 (New King James Version).

Jesus, Lover of My Soul
Words by Charles Wesley, 1740

Jesus, lover of my soul,
Let me to Thy bosom fly,
While the nearer waters roll,
While the tempest still is high:
Hide me, O my Savior, hide,
Till the storm of life is past;
Safe into the haven guide,
O receive my soul at last!

Other refuge have I none,
Hangs my helpless soul on Thee;
Leave, ah! leave me not alone,
Still support and comfort me!
All my trust on Thee is stayed,
All my help from Thee I bring;
Cover my defenseless head
With the shadow of Thy wing.

Thou, O Christ, art all I want;
More than all in Thee I find:
Raise the fallen, cheer the faint,
Heal the sick, and lead the blind.
Just and holy is Thy name;
I am all unrighteousness;
False and full of sin I am,
Thou art full of truth and grace.

Plenteous grace with Thee is found,
Grace to cover all my sin;
Let the healing streams abound;
Make and keep me pure within:
Thou of life the fountain art;
Freely let me take of Thee;
Spring Thou up within my heart,
Rise to all eternity.[12]

12. Charles Wesley, "Jesus, Lover of My Soul," in *Hymns and Sacred Poems* (London: Strahan, 1740), 174–76.

Chapter 2

The Prodigal Daughter

by Angie Ahmed-Galal's wife

"And He (Jesus) looked around to see her who had done this thing. But the woman, fearing and trembling, knowing what had happened to her, came and fell down before Him and told Him the whole truth. And He said to her, "DAUGHTER, your faith has made you well. Go in peace, and be healed of your affliction." Mark 5:32-34[1]

A Childhood of Instability

IN THE SPRING OF 1980, a young and newly married girl gave birth. She was only 16 and married less than a year. Her husband, a young Mexican man, had only been in America a few short years. He fell in love with a young girl that was hitching a ride on the side of the road. In no time at all, they were married. Partly because of love and partly out of fear of her parents and a gun. When they were wed, she already had one daughter. In no time at all, they welcomed me (Angie Ahmed), a pink baby girl. Even though my dark-skinned father was expecting a darker-skinned baby boy. Exactly two years later, they welcomed a baby boy, my brother. Only a few short years after they were married, they separated. This was the beginning of me and my siblings unstable and difficult childhood. Really, it was my brother and

1. Mark 5:32-34 (New King James Version).

me. My older sister was mostly raised by our grandparents. Not to say her life wasn't difficult. She just wasn't usually with us.

Most of my memories from when I was very young are unpleasant. This isn't to say my childhood was completely awful. It's only that I don't recall a bunch of happy moments. For starters, we moved a lot. Not just from town to town but also state to state. Over the years, I have joked, saying my mother was part gypsy, seeming to not be content in one place for too long. The reality was, in a lot of cases, she ran from problems. Most of her problems were men. In the first seventeen years of my life, she had been married four times. This does not include other men she did not marry. They passed through our lives like the wind. Telling you all this isn't to talk terribly of my mother. It's only to give a rough idea of what life was like. She couldn't have known the impact it would have on my brother and myself. Since we grew up with such instability, I knew I wanted to provide stability for my kids, if I ever had any. As much as I loved my mother, I did not want to be like her. Not in this way anyhow. In other ways, I am exceedingly thankful to be just like her.

A Cycle of Sin

Fast-forward, at the age of sixteen, I moved from North Carolina to Florida to live with my boyfriend. Before I moved to be with him, I was living with one of my mother's ex-husbands. When I got there, he had a place for us right beside my mother and her boyfriend. It's going to be no shocker to tell you, soon after, I was pregnant. I was three years older than my own mother when she first became pregnant. In my arrogance, I thought I had done so much better than her. I gave birth to my first son two weeks after I turned 17. His father and I did not last even to his birth.

At the age of eighteen, I met a navy guy while working at Waffle House. We were together only a short time before he went on a six-month deployment. I found out I was pregnant almost immediately after he left. When he returned from sea, we got married. Another month after we married, my second son arrived. At the time of his birth, I was nineteen years old. Five months later, we moved to Virginia from Florida, where he was being stationed. Shortly after the move, I was with child again.

This time was different. This time, I had a toddler and a baby. This time, we were in a new place and knew no one. This time, we couldn't even begin to imagine how we would be able to take care of another baby. To this point in my life, several tragic things had happened to me. But nothing had prepared me for that. To this day, I cry over it as I reflect on the reality: I murdered my own baby. And I tried to justify it. Only months after my wicked deed, I was pregnant again. I wouldn't be able to tell you why things were different, but they were. And at the age of twenty, I welcomed my third baby into the world, a sweet baby girl.

My husband and I truly did try to make marriage work. But we had no idea of how or why to do that. We were both selfish but in very different ways. We were both at fault for the failure of our marriage. When our youngest began elementary school, our years of on-again, off-again separation began. I moved out well before we formally divorced. On my 30th birthday is when our divorce was final.

The Sin of Selfishness

Before I ever divorced my then-husband, I met another man. In the years of our relationship, I became pregnant twice. In my selfishness and fear, I had two more abortions. The first, the father knew about. The second, I had done without his knowledge or agreement. To make matters worse, I used the information like a knife to stab him in the heart. And of course, he and I also did not stay together. For years it was difficult in many ways. We both had three children we had been raising together for years. His younger two boys were very close to my boys. To this day, I think of his boys often. To me, they were like my own boys. Even though I was not their mother.

After our real break, I dated several men. I worked nonstop, and I partied hard. In my mind, I was a good mother. Since I worked hard to support them and they didn't lack anything, so I thought. My children were intelligent, talented, and kind. I did not have a ton of problems with them. Until my oldest got in a bad way in high school. I used to think he was a foolish boy that couldn't stay out of trouble. Over time, I realized he wasn't the foolish one; it was me. I had failed him! I failed all my children. Especially the ones I had murdered in my womb. But this knowledge still eluded me for some time.

A Look in God's Mirror

When I was 34, my heart had been deeply broken again. Still, this was not new to me. I forced myself to create an online dating account. There was a man I was interested in, and I decided to go on a date. I met him at a Mexican restaurant. He was handsome, bold, and charismatic. But he was also gentle, kind, and patient. Our first meeting was at the end of January. We continued to see each other through February. It would be nice to say it was some special deep love. Truth was, it was like my other relationships, based on lust. The last week of February, we went away for a couple of days. It was then I started to realize things I did not know about him. Things started to make more sense. Already, I knew he didn't drink, smoke, swear, or in general act a fool. He was most always calm and collected. And now I started to realize why. He was a Christian.

At first, the new information didn't mean much to me. It was just another layer of his strangeness as far as I was concerned. Then, of course, things began to change. The week following our weekend away, I came to his home to make us dinner. This was the first week of March.

While standing in his dining room, he asked me, "Angie, what do you think happens when we die?"

This question caught me off guard. Regardless of the time spent in church, I wasn't used to such serious talks about the afterlife. Still, I did have an uninformed opinion. And I replied, "I think like most people do, you either go to heaven or hell."

He replied, "Where do you think you will go?"

Thinking so highly of myself, I answer, "Heaven, of course!"

He continued and simply asked me, "Why?"

What a silly question, I thought, and said, "You know me a little bit by now, I am a really good person."

The man continued with his line of questioning. "May I give you the good person test?" he asked.

"Of course!" I quickly responded.

He starts with, "Have you ever lied?"

"Of course I have," I said, thinking, haven't we all?

Next, he asked, "Have you ever stolen anything?"

My mind immediately thought back to my teen years, where I stole from stores like it was my job. And I simply answered, "Yes."

Next, he asks, "Have you ever taken God's name in vain?"

At the time, I did not understand the seriousness of it. But I knew I was terribly guilty. I almost did not have a vocabulary apart from blaspheming God's holy name. Then again, I simply answered, "Yes."

Lastly, he asked me, "Have you ever committed adultery?"

Well, I was again deeply guilty of this. He obviously knew it, as we had been engaging in these acts together. For the fourth time, I admitted, "I am guilty."

He looked at me with such sincerity and said, "So when you stand before God on judgment day, by your own admission, you will be a lying, thieving, blaspheming, adulterer. Will you go to heaven or hell?"

It was then I knew the truth: I was guilty before God. With all seriousness, I answered, "Hell."

Next, he asked me, "What will you say to God in your defense?"

I thought about it, and as a rare occasion in my life, I didn't have anything to say. I quietly responded, "I don't know."

My mind was intrigued, and my heart was being softened. After realizing such terrible, bad news—that I was guilty before a Holy Just God—the man continued with the most amazing thing I had ever heard. He proceeded with the Gospel, explaining to me that Jesus Christ was born of a virgin, making Him fully man and fully God, a representative of both God and man.[2] He lived a perfect, sinless life, always being obedient to the Father.[3] He willingly went to the cross as a sacrifice for those whom the Father had given Him.[4] His last words were "Tetelestai"; in English, we say, "It is finished," but it means the penalty has been paid in full.[5] He died and was buried. Three days later, He rose from the dead, showing the Father had been pleased with His sacrifice.[6] Now, He sits at the right hand of the Father.[7]

A New Heart and a New Life

Wow, this blew my mind! But what did this mean for me? I already believed Jesus died for sinners, even though I didn't understand its true implications. Once upon a time, I asked Jesus into my heart. Now I realized it didn't mean anything. What does asking Jesus into your heart even do or mean? The answer is, Nothing! I realized it as he continued in our talk. He told me salvation was two sides of one coin. Repentance—turning from sin, not just

2. Matthew 1:23; John 1:14 (New King James Version).

3. Hebrews 4:15; John 8:29 (New King James Version).

4. John 10:11, 17-18 (New King James Version).

5. John 19:30 (New King James Version).

6. 1 Corinthians 15:3-4 (New King James Version).

7. Hebrews 1:3 (New King James Version).

being sorry but grieving over it because it's against God and letting go of it (Romans 3:23).[8] Faith—trusting in Christ and His work of redemption alone (John 14:6).[9] There is nothing I can do to save myself. All our "good" deeds are like filthy rags to the Lord (Isaiah 64:6).[10] Jesus Christ is the only sufficient sacrifice (Hebrews 10:12).[11] I could not believe what I was hearing. These are things no one ever told me in church. As our conversation wound down, we sat quietly and watched my first-ever "Christian" movie, Fireproof.[12] The movie ended. I kissed him on the cheek and said goodbye.

I had the most awful night of sleep. There was one thing the man had said I couldn't stop thinking about. At one point, he told me, "When we say we are good, we are comparing ourselves to God. Even Jesus told the rich young ruler, only God is good (Matthew 19:16-22)."[13] So, I just kept thinking, I think I am like God. That's when I realized I had made myself my own god. Letting go of this thought was impossible. Bright and early in the morning, I messaged the man. Standing in front of my brewing coffee, I asked, "Why did we have that conversation last night?

His response was quick and said, "Before I can have a right relationship with you or my other friends or my family or anyone else, first, I must have my relationship right with God." These are the last words I read as an unbeliever. Immediately afterward, it was as if a ton of bricks fell on me, and I was crushed. In an instant, I knew everything about my life was wrong. Everything about my life was rooted in sin. With the snap of a finger, I knew I was a terrible mother. I knew I had a work problem, a man problem, and a drinking problem. And by problem, I mean I was deep in sin. I started to cry and pray. Yet, I have no idea to this day what I prayed. Also, I did not know what had just happened to me. Nor did I know how drastically my life would change.

After I collected myself, I responded, "I agree, now what?"

He told me we could only be friends, and I said, "Okay."

Everything was different now. I had conviction over sin and a thirst for God's word. I had gone to my children and asked for forgiveness. Of course,

8. Romans 3:23 (New King James Version).

9. John 14:6 (New King James Version).

10. Isaiah 64:6 (New King James Version).

11. Hebrews 10:12 (New King James Version).

12. Fireproof, directed by Alex Kendrick (Albany, GA: Sherwood Pictures, 2008), DVD.

13. Matthew 19:16-22 (New King James Version

they said yes but they didn't understand. That's when I finally realized I was just like my mother. I finally realized my children had been suffering at my own hands. Of all my "problems" this was the worst. I really did think I was a good mom. The truth is I was terrible. Sure, I provided for them things like, food, water, shelter, clothes etc. . But what about the most important things? What about unconditional love, patience, understanding, or even just physically being there for them. I could of and should have done so much more for them. They needed a better mother, but they got me.

A New Creation

My new friend bought me a Bible. All I could do was talk about everything I was learning. It was and is the most amazing news. I thought surely everyone would want to know about it. At work, I went from the girl everyone was afraid to upset, as I was in a somewhat leadership position and I was very harsh and strict in my rule-following, to a girl that wanted to share the good news of Jesus Christ. At home, my children were glad I had been softened. At the same time, I must have seemed like a completely different person. At my main job, especially, it quickly became clear how not everyone wanted to hear about my good news. While I did maintain a few close relationships, most of the people I called friends now mostly shunned me, as well as talked about me behind my back. I am not an easily offended person, yet, it was hard to swallow. It did make sense. I was drastically different. My desires and thoughts had changed almost overnight. Everything truly was different, and I couldn't go back.

As for my friend who God used to draw me to Himself, for a few months, we were just friends. Then he asked me to be his girlfriend (as silly as it sounds). A few months after that, he asked me to be his wife. God had used what we meant for evil to be for my good and His glory. He not only used our deep sin to save me, but He also gave me Galal to be my husband. I cannot comprehend or explain the great extent of God's mercy and grace in my life. The fact that God took a woman who was a terrible mother, adulterer, murderer of her own babies, and just all-around wicked and transformed her into someone who can be patient, gentle, kind, and desiring to do for others just because. Not that I do these things well, but it is my great desire now to honor the God that saved me. To be a proper representative of the great transformation He has done on the inside of me. Ezekiel 36:26 says: "I will give you a new heart and put a new spirit within you; I will take the heart of stone out of your flesh and give you a heart of flesh."[14]

Praise be to God for doing the work in me that I could have never done myself!

14. Ezekiel 36:26 (New King James Version).

When I Survey the Wondrous Cross

Words by Isaac Watts, 1707

When I survey the wondrous cross
On which the Prince of glory died,
My richest gain I count but loss,
And pour contempt on all my pride.

Forbid it, Lord, that I should boast,
Save in the death of Christ my God;
All the vain things that charm me most,
I sacrifice them to His blood.

See, from His head, His hands, His feet,
Sorrow and love flow mingled down;
Did e'er such love and sorrow meet,
Or thorns compose so rich a crown?

Were the whole realm of nature mine,
That were a present far too small;
Love so amazing, so divine,
Demands my soul, my life, my all.[15]

15. Isaac Watts, "When I Survey the Wondrous Cross," in *Hymns and Spiritual Songs* (London: J. Lawrence, 1707), 138–40.

Chapter 3

Charismatic Chaos No More

"I cannot endure false doctrine, however neatly it may be put before me. Would you have me eat poisoned meat because the dish is of the choicest ware? It makes me indignant when I hear another gospel put before the people with enticing words, by men who would fain make merchandise of souls; and I marvel at those who have soft words for such deceivers." Charles Spurgeon[1]

Deceived by Charlatans

THE YEAR WAS 1994. My mother and I were headed off to a Benny Hinn crusade. I was a little lad in the 6th grade, but I still remember that event vividly. Mr. Hinn was one of her favorites. We arrived at the stadium where the event was being held, and it was packed. I have never seen so many people gathered together in one place in all my life. The music was loud and repetitive, almost hypnotic-like.

After maybe an hour or so, this Middle Eastern-looking man came out in a white suit. He grabbed the microphone and began to speak. His voice immediately grabbed my attention. He was very likable and charming. As a little boy, I would watch him on TBN with my mother. I was fascinated as I watched him wave his jacket around at people, like he was a Jedi Knight

1. Charles H. Spurgeon, "The Old, Old Story," in The Metropolitan Tabernacle Pulpit Sermons, vol. 10 (London: Passmore & Alabaster, 1864), 325.

with a lightsaber, as he knocked people down with some sort of supernatural power. There is actually a YouTube video where someone put a lightsaber in his hand as he knocked people down with every strike. It is pretty funny. It is called, "Benny Hinn Sith Lord (Improved Sound)."[2]

I remember watching a section to the right of me of 100 people or so way up in the stands. He began speaking and pointing their way and talked about the power of the Holy Spirit that was about to fall upon them. And then he would shout, "TAKE IT", as he waved his hand towards that section, and you saw every single one of them fall back into their seats. I really thought that was the power of God. My mom did too. He would bring people up on the stage and claim to heal them all as he waved his hands and jacket around, yelling, "TAKE IT." Then they would bring up all the wheelchairs later on in the service of all the people who supposedly got healed during the 3-4 hour service. Then when it was all over, we went home, and life was back to normal. Apparently, the power of the Spirit never seemed to last once the music and show was over.

A Mother's Love Amidst Errors

False teachers hurt people. Growing up, my mother was sold out. I didn't know any better myself. I thought this is what Christianity was all about. Nevertheless, mothers are a gift from the Lord. I had and still have the best mother ever! She did everything for me growing up. She didn't know or believe the gospel, so I never heard that from her, but through God's common grace, I learned some true things that have stuck with me to this day.

I got a lot of spankings as a child. I remember asking one time, "Mom, why do you spank me?"

She would say, "Because God tells me to. I should be spanking you with a rod because that is what the Bible says. I spank you because I love you."

From a very young age, I was taught that if the Bible said it, that settled it. It was God's Word after all. I am so thankful to her for teaching me that. I used to tell my friends who never got spankings that their parents didn't love them. They would argue back and say, "Yes they do!"

I would say, "Well, the Bible says if you love your children, you will spank them. If you don't love them, you won't. My mom spanks me a lot

2. "Benny Hinn Sith Lord (Improved Sound)," YouTube video, 2:45, posted by "Derrick," February 25, 2008, https://www.youtube.com/watch?v=5lvU-Dislhc.

because she loves me." Proverbs 13:24 says, "He who spares his rod hates his son, But he who loves him disciplines him promptly."[3]

Confronting Error

After the Lord saved me, it changed our relationship. We still loved each other and were close, but we no longer bonded over false teaching. I couldn't stand to listen to all the preachers she loved. Whether it was Perry Stone, Jonathan Cahn, or Jesse Duplantis, I could no longer stomach their teaching. It made me sick to my stomach and angry. My mom's feelings and experiences were her ultimate authority. They were the lens on her glasses, which she would wear as she read through her Bible.

I remember having several conversations after my conversion with her, and they would go something like this. "Galal, would you please watch this? I recorded it for you."

I would respond, "Okay, mom." Then while I was watching it or after having watched it, I would tell her why I disagree, and I would share Scripture to explain why. My mother used to get so frustrated with me when I did that. Not because I was being mean or rude. It was because every time we would talk about God, she would say something that wasn't true, and I would simply ask her, "Mom, where does the Bible teach that?" That was it. . . She would get upset, and then we would talk about something else. I let her borrow a book once called Charismatic Chaos by John MacArthur.[4] As she read it, she got so angry that she stopped and gave it back to me. I asked her what she didn't agree with, but she couldn't articulate it, because her objection wasn't coming from the Bible.

I thought my mom was a Christian, but she wasn't. She actually believed in another gospel, which is no gospel at all, just ask Paul: "I marvel that you are turning away so soon from Him who called you in the grace of Christ, to a different gospel, which is not another; but there are some who trouble you and want to pervert the gospel of Christ. But even if we, or an angel from heaven, preach any other gospel to you than what we have preached to you, let him be accursed. As we have said before, so now I say again, if anyone preaches any other gospel to you than what you have received, let him be accursed" (Galatians 1:6-9).[5]

3. Proverbs 13:24 (New King James Version).
4. John MacArthur, Charismatic Chaos (Grand Rapids: Zondervan, 1992).
5. Galatians 1:6-9 (New King James Version).

She was infatuated with "prophecy" or "people who had a new word from the Lord" or "someone who took another trip to heaven," etc. I kept explaining to her that God's Word is sufficient for all of life and godliness. That God in times past spoke to us in many ways (such as in dreams, or visions, through donkeys or burning bushes), but in these last days, He has spoken to us in His Son (Hebrews 1:1-2).[6] The Bible is the final speaking of God.

A Mother's True Conversion

One day, she texted me out of nowhere and told me she was wrong. I asked, "Wrong about what?"

She said, "Wrong about EVERYTHING she believed about the Bible!" She asked me if I have ever seen a YouTube video called "Clouds without Water" by Justin Peters.[7] I laughed and told her that I have been trying to get her to watch that video for years. She said that God saved her! I was blown away. Here is my mama, in her 60s, and now she is truly saved. She has been born again! Praise the Lord!

Not only did God truly save her, but she immediately became Reformed, which is just another way of saying she was biblical about EVERYTHING (even believer's baptism). She would ask me questions about everything she was reading in the Bible. She still does, and I love it! She also went from being a Charismatic to a Cessationist overnight. That right there is proof of God's existence! She went from singing songs like "I expect a miracle today" to singing songs like "I Asked the Lord That I Might Grow," which is her favorite now.

One of her favorite doctrines is the Sovereignty of God. According to the Second London Baptist Confession of Faith, it says, "God has decreed in Himself from all eternity, by the most wise and holy counsel of His own will, freely and unchangeably, all things which shall ever come to pass."[8] It truly was the most amazing thing I have ever witnessed. She had lots of questions about Eschatology (study of last things), about the

---

6. Hebrews 1:1-2 (New King James Version).

7. Justin Peters, "Clouds without Water," YouTube video, 2:03:45, posted by "Justin Peters Ministries," July 15, 2014, https://www.youtube.com/watch?v=2lOnr7nmd9g.

8. Second London Baptist Confession of Faith (1689), chap. 3, para. 1, in A Faith to Confess: The Baptist Confession of Faith of 1689 (Leeds: Carey Publications, 1975), 12.

Church and Israel, etc. She now holds the biblical position on Eschatology. . . Amillennialism, of course!

Seeing the change in my mom was so amazing. Why do good things happen to bad people like my mom? Because Jesus is full of grace and truth! He loves to save sinners! When God saved my mom, He was putting His grace on display for all to see. She will be a trophy of His grace for all of eternity right next to me. "Oh, the depth of the riches both of the wisdom and knowledge of God! How unsearchable are His judgments and His ways past finding out!" (Romans 11:33).[9]

This, however, did not help her marriage. My parents met at Wyatt's Cafeteria in 1981. My dad was in the states from Cairo on a work visa. So when they met, he was a Muslim, and my mother was a professing Christian. In reality, she was a false convert. They dated for about 5 months before they decided to get married. The problem was trying to get married. My mom was not about to have a Muslim ceremony, called a Nikah. My mom's pastor at the time also refused to perform the ceremony. So they ended up going to the courthouse to get married.

The one area of major conflict in their marriage early on was religion, as you would expect. My dad said to my mom after I was born, "You will not take my son into a church."

To which she responded with, "We will go to church every Sunday!" They had many other arguments about it and still do to this day. But when my mother became a real Christian, things got significantly worse. Jesus did tell us that is what we are to expect, did He not? In Matthew 10:34-39, He said, "Do not think that I came to bring peace on earth. I did not come to bring peace but a sword. For I have come to set a man against his father, a daughter against her mother, and a daughter-in-law against her mother-in-law; and a man's enemies will be those of his own household. He who loves father or mother more than Me is not worthy of Me. And he who loves son or daughter more than Me is not worthy of Me. And he who does not take his cross and follow after Me is not worthy of Me. He who finds his life will lose it, and he who loses his life for My sake will find it."[10]

My mother has been such an encouragement to me through it all. She has a servant's heart. She has served my dad and still does to this day like no one else I have ever known. Elisabeth Elliot once said, "If you want to find out if you have the heart of a servant, you will find out when you are

9. Romans 11:33 (New King James Version).
10. Matthew 10:34-39 (New King James Version).

treated like one."[11] Well, my mom has been treated like a servant time and time again, and I have never once heard her complain about it. I have seen God's grace in her, and I praise Him for that!

1 Peter 3:3-4 comes to mind when I think about her, where Peter is speaking to wives: "Do not let your adornment be merely outward—arranging the hair, wearing gold, or putting on fine apparel—rather let it be the hidden person of the heart, with the incorruptible beauty of a gentle and quiet spirit, which is very precious in the sight of God."[12] God saved my mother, a very self-righteous older lady. Why? Because He loves to save sinners! Is that fair? No, it is grace. "Ah Lord God! Behold, You have made the heavens and the earth by Your great power and by Your outstretched arm! Nothing is too difficult for You!" (Jeremiah 32:17, NASB).[13] Now that my mother truly loves the Lord and is one of His daughters, the song, "I Asked the Lord That I Might Grow," has become her greatest desire.

11. Elisabeth Elliot, Keep a Quiet Heart (Ann Arbor: Servant Publications, 1995), 189.

12. 1 Peter 3:3-4 (New King James Version).

13. Jeremiah 32:17 (New American Standard Bible).

I Asked the Lord That I Might Grow
Written by John Newton, 1779

I asked the Lord that I might grow
In faith and love and ev'ry grace,
Might more of His salvation know,
And seek more earnestly His face.

'Twas He who taught me thus to pray,
And He, I trust, has answered prayer,
But it has been in such a way
As almost drove me to despair.

I hoped that in some favored hour
At once He'd answer my request
And, by His love's constraining pow'r,
Subdue my sins and give me rest.

Instead of this, He made me feel
The hidden evils of my heart
And let the angry pow'rs of hell
Assault my soul in ev'ry part.

Yea, more with His own hand He seemed
Intent to aggravate my woe,
Crossed all the fair designs I schemed,
Humbled my heart and laid me low.

"Lord, why is this," I trembling cried;
"Wilt Thou pursue Thy worm to death?"
"'Tis in this way," the Lord replied,
"I answer prayer for grace and faith."

"These inward trials I employ
From self and pride to set thee free
And break thy schemes of earthly joy
That thou may'st find thy all in Me."[14]

---

14. John Newton, "I Asked the Lord That I Might Grow," in Olney Hymns (London: W. Oliver, 1779), no. 36.

Chapter 4

My Mother, Now My Sister

by Angie Ahmed-Galal's wife

"Now when the Pharisee who had invited Him saw this, he spoke to himself, saying, 'This Man, if He were a prophet, would know who and what manner of woman this is who is touching Him, for she is a sinner.'" Luke 7:39[1]

WHEN I TOLD MY husband Galal I would write this story, I didn't realize how challenging it would be. Not because I don't know the story. But because, how do I represent someone rightly that can't correct me? And of all people, my mother. I want to honor her memory while also being honest about who she was. I pray I can do both. And that God will use her story to further glorify Himself.

As I start writing this chapter, it's the day before Easter Sunday, aka Resurrection Day. It reminds me of when I was young. My mother would go all out for Easter. She would do elaborate baskets, brand new outfits for the occasion, Easter egg hunts, sometimes scavenger hunts. And my most favorite thing was this huge peanut butter chocolate-covered egg. They would have our names written on them in frosting. They were the most delicious things. She really went out of her way to make it special. I have no idea why Easter was such a big deal to her. Remembering this brings tears to my eyes. When I wrote my own story, I had forgotten all about it.

1. Luke 7:39 (New King James Version).

Most of my memories are not pleasant. How could I have let those sweet memories slip through my mind? Personally, I think it's easy to forget the sweet memories when there are so many painful ones. I don't want to remember my mother for just the hard times. But I want to remember her in her fullness, the sweet and the painful.

A Jackie of All Trades

My mother Edy was a beautiful woman. She had long brown hair and bright blue eyes. It was obvious why men were drawn to her. And if you knew my mother, it would make even more sense why they hung around. She wasn't just beautiful but intelligent, hardworking, and kind. She was the kind of person that seemed to be able to fix anything and everything. My mom was a Jackie of all trades. Some of her career choices were nurse, waitress, real estate manager, exotic entertainer, and truck driver. It makes me laugh thinking of the drastic difference between her choices. But it's just the way she was. A lady who wanted to know how to do a lot of things and be good at them all. As she often was good at whatever she did.

While my mom was amazing, she was also terribly difficult. Running from man to man and state to state. When I was young, I didn't understand. She worked hard to provide for us. I knew it wasn't because she needed a man to help her. Now that I am older and have unknowingly lived a similar life to my mother, I know it was most likely out of loneliness. Not that it's an excuse. It just makes sense to me now. I always saw her as such a strong lady. You weren't likely to see her cry. If you did, you knew there was a serious problem. Likely, I could count on one hand how many times I witnessed it myself. The reality was it was all a facade. She was fragile on the inside like the rest of us. Her exterior was tough. And yet she was still a normal human being with emotions. Not the heartless mother I often mistook her for as a young person.

A Newfound Relationship

When the Lord saved me, she and I were not very close. We did talk on occasion. Mostly the conversations were shallow and brief. And often she caught me up on family drama. After I realized what had truly happened to me (God redeeming me), I was ecstatic to tell her. I was also excited to share the gospel with her. To my surprise, my mom was relieved to hear

I was a Christian. It had kind of caught me off guard. It wasn't because she was worried about my soul. Instead, she had been worried about my hardcore drinking habits. But she never mentioned it to me before. It also kind of shocked me. Not just because she never brought it up before but also because it was so motherly of her. She spent a lot of time being worried about my brother, as he was her baby. And little time being worried about me (so I thought). Regardless, it was the beginning of a newfound relationship between us.

My husband and I shared the gospel with my mother several times over the years. She was never hostile to it and often had good questions. Growing up, she did go to church a bit. And she told me she had never heard the gospel as we explained it before. Over time, she started using "Christian" lingo like, Lord willing. Occasionally, she would call me with an epiphany she had. Once she called me and said she realized she had made an idol of Mark (her then-boyfriend). Another time she called and said our whole family was going to hell. She would listen to sermons I sent and call with spiritual questions. A few times she called wanting us to find her a church to visit. And we did every time, but she never went.

Speaking Truth in Love

As tough as my mom was, she had several health problems. I wanted to be there for her as much as possible. And so, if I had the opportunity to love her practically, I took it. One of the times she needed surgery on some veins in her legs, I took the trip from Virginia to Florida to be with her. Sitting in the living room, we watched the "Exit" movie by Living Waters. It's a movie about suicide, and my mother was moved by it. It was a topic she was very familiar with, and so she wanted to share it.[2] A little while later, we sat out on the front porch while she smoked a cigarette. Since she was moved by the movie, I took the opportunity to say some hard truths. By now, my mom had been professing Christ for a long time. And yet there was NO fruit. What I tell you next will seem harsh. But I couldn't let my mother go on deceiving herself.

And so, I said to her, "Mom, I cannot know your heart. Really, that is between you and the Lord. But Scripture is clear we can have a good indication by our fruit. And if I am looking at you, you don't have good fruit. You

2. Exit: The Appeal of Suicide, directed by Ray Comfort (Santa Clarita, CA: Living Waters Publications, 2016), DVD.

have bad fruit indicating you are of the devil." Even with those hard words, she didn't get angry at me but just listened. Before heading home, I pleaded with her once more and said, "I love you."

As time passed, things with my mother did not change. She still professed Christ, and she still lived in obvious sin with no contrition over it. The only thing that did change was our relationship. It continued to grow stronger. We talked more frequently, and we had meaningful conversations. When I went into labor and gave birth at 29 weeks' gestation, she rushed to my side. Even in an unconverted state, it was a sweet time in our relationship. It really felt like I had a loving mother.

The Dreaded C Word

About four months after I had my preemie daughter, my mom called me. She said, "Diane, I have something to tell you. You know how the doctors thought I had pneumonia and checked for fluid on my lungs. It's not pneumonia. The doctor says I have stage 2 lung cancer."

All I could say was, "I am coming." That's exactly what I did. I packed up my preemie daughter and myself and headed to Florida. That was in January of 2019. I spent the better part of the next five months taking care of her as best I could. Sometimes I would fly back to Virginia for appointments for my baby girl, Tulip. And sometimes my husband would come down to be with us all. It was a difficult and yet sweet time. The Lord really used that time to knit our hearts together as mother and daughter even tighter.

In May, I had gone back home to Virginia for a short time. When I returned to Florida, my mom had just been released from the hospital. It was the third time she had been admitted in the five months. She looked at me and said, "I will come live with you." I had been asking her if she would please consider moving to Virginia with us. The hospital and important doctors she needed were only five minutes away, unlike the hour drive to each appointment we had been trekking. Her saying she would move was a huge relief to me. We packed up what she needed, took care of technical issues like records, and headed to Virginia. The trip was tremendously painful for her. As soon as we reached Virginia, she was immediately admitted to the hospital. About a week later, she was released again.

In the Midst of Darkness LIGHT

A few days later, she had her first oncologist appointment. We expected it to be like all the other ones we had already had. Sitting there with the doctor, he went over her record. It was not like the other visits. He told us information we hadn't been told before. His talk with us was very thorough. At the end of his walkthrough, he looked at my mother and said, "I know you were diagnosed with stage 2, but now you are either stage 3b or stage 4. Because the cancer has spread to your other lung and is moving through your body." I can only imagine how terrified my mom was in that moment. My heart seemed to sink into a pit. Then the doctor continued, "There is no coming back from this. All we can do is try to prolong your life." Somehow, my mother kept her composure and told the doctor she would like to live as long as possible. He informed us of his intention on how to do it, and we left.

When we got home, we watched part of "The American Gospel."[3] My mother was, of course, very tired and went to lay down. A while later, I went to check on her. I saw a look on her face I had never seen before: fear. I quietly sat beside her in a chair. She looked at me with tears in her eyes and said, "Angie, you are always telling me to cry out to God and ask for help. But I don't know how to do that. How do I do that, how do I ask God for help?"

My feelings were mixed over the question. I was glad to hear her ask, yet scared she only expected God to miraculously heal her. I started out talking about why we go to God. I wanted to make sure she understood God can, of course, heal her. But it's not why we run to Him. We do so because we are guilty before Him. Because all our sin is against Him, a Holy Righteous God. After trying to be as clear as possible with her, I called for Galal. He proceeded to walk my mother through the law for what seemed like the 100th time. Then he shared the gospel with her for the 100th time. Last, he asked her if she wanted to pray, and she said yes. He started off praying for her first. When she began to pray out loud, tears immediately ran down her face. Through sobs, my mom started confessing sin to God and pleading for forgiveness. She was specific and sincere. She confessed sin she had even denied for years. My mind was blown;

---

3. American Gospel: Christ Alone, directed by Brandon Kimber (Transition Studios, 2018), streaming.

I couldn't believe what was happening. My mother, of all people, now wasn't just my mother but my sister.

You Will Know Them by Their Fruit

Since we didn't know how much time she had left, we decided to rent a beach house for a week. Anyone who could make it was welcome. Both my brother and sister and some of their children made it. Her older sister Mickey, one of my cousins Chris, and his wife, as well as Mark, her now-fiancé, all made it to spend some time with her. Before they arrived, my mother asked Galal and me to please share the gospel with them. While we were all there, she called my brother Bruce, sister Mary, and me into her room. And for the first time in my life, she apologized to us. She confessed to being a terrible mother and asked for forgiveness. It was a beautiful moment to behold. My tough and prideful mother was now gentle and humble. Before the week had ended, my mother was back in the hospital.

My mom was in a really bad way. Her body wasn't well enough to fight off infections or heal. Then her heart started to have problems. They trans-ferred her to the heart hospital. After they moved her, she became septic. In the meantime, she would call and ask us to come have a Bible study. She also called and asked us to bring my gospel booklets. The ones she had, she had already given away to the nurses. My mom was finally bearing good fruit. To this day, I believe it was the kindness of the Lord for me, to comfort me for what was to come. One such booklet, titled "Don't Stub Your Toe," was among those she distributed.[4]

Gone to Glory

The morning of July 25th, my mother called me from the hospital. Her body was drained, and she wanted to be left alone. She asked me to call everyone and tell them not to bother her. I said, "Of course," made my calls, and changed my plans of going up there. It wasn't a big deal because she was coming home in the next couple of days, according to the doctors. July 26th arrived, and before I was out of bed, the phone rang. This time, it was one of her doctors. She told me to get to the hospital immediately because my mother's body was in its last stages of life. I quickly hung up and, with

4. Todd Friel, Don't Stub Your Toe (Fortis Institute, 2017), gospel booklet.

my shaking hands, called my husband, grabbed my baby girl, and jumped in my car. As fast as I could, I started calling everyone. It's the most awful thing, telling everyone, "Mom is in her last stages of life."

When I got to the hospital, my mom was still lucid. I got to hug and kiss her, even though she was still considered septic. They gave her the medicine to help relax her body. After that, she didn't have any more coherent speech. Her fiancé Mark somehow made it from Florida to Virginia before she passed. My brother was on his way. He still called to tell her he loved her. My mom wasn't having conversations, but I believe she was listening. People kept calling, so I kept putting the phone to her ear. My sister Mary, my mom's oldest, called. She was the last person my mom hadn't heard from. I put the phone to her ear, and my sister talked. Shortly after Mary called, my mother took her last breath.

While the doctors were in the room, I stood just outside the door. Beside me was one of the nurses' carts. On it was a "Don't Stub Your Toe" gospel booklet. It was one of the gospel booklets my mother had been giving out. At that moment, a smile came to my face. The Lord reminded me: I would see her again. This wasn't the end; our separation was temporary. I was terribly sad at the same time thankful. God did something only He could do. The most miraculous thing He did was reconcile us both to Himself. A close second was that He reconciled a mother and daughter to each other. He used an awful situation for not just my mom's good but mine also and His glory!

Praise be to God!

In the Shane and Shane song "Though You Slay Me,"[5] The chorus talks about how we respond when trials come. How we praise God no matter our circumstances. Let this always be my heart's posture in the midst of grief.

---

5. Shane Barnard and Shane Everett, "Though You Slay Me," Bring Your Nothing, Fair Trade Services, 2013, compact disc.

Chapter 5

Entrusted with the King's Daughter

"Houses and riches are an inheritance from fathers, but a prudent wife is from the LORD." Proverbs 19:14[1]

The Proposal

IT WAS A CRISP November morning in 2014. I woke up with a smile on my face. After all my planning, I was ready to propose to Angie. We had been dating for 3 months at that point. I knew I loved her and wanted to marry her before we even started dating. Some say we were dating before I asked her to be my girlfriend. One of those people was my best friend, Sean Lewis. He would joke with me all the time before I asked her out, by saying, "What do you say people are doing that go on dates? Dating!"

A couple of weeks prior, Angie and I were at the airport picking someone up. While we were waiting, we looked around in the gift shop. I saw some rings, so I walked over and started looking at them. I was trying to be clever, hoping she would come over and do the same. She did! I asked her which ones she liked. During our conversation, I THOUGHT I heard her say she wears a size 6. Boy, was I wrong. . .

Later that week, I went to the mall to buy a ring for her. I knew she didn't really care about diamond rings because they were so expensive, so I found a ring with a crystal in it. It was something GALAL liked, so I thought she would like it too. I was operating in the normative principle

1. Proverbs 19:14 (New King James Version).

instead of the regulative. I got her what GALAL likes instead of what AN-GIE likes. Big mistake! Regulative Principle all day, fellows! When you get your wife a gift, get her what SHE likes, not what YOU like.

After getting the ring, I had it all planned out. She was a waitress at Pocahontas, a breakfast restaurant on the oceanfront. I used to stop by from time to time and bring her flowers. So, I came up with the ingenious plan of proposing to her at work. I asked my family and her 3 children to all meet for breakfast that morning. I stopped and got some flowers on my way. I had the ring and also got some coffee for her, upon her request. I was dressed to impress, as you can imagine. I put on my finest jeans, with a button-up and my sports coat. I was looking sharp and smelling good with my Acqua Di Gio on.

I arrived at the restaurant about 9:15 that morning. Everybody was there waiting for me. I walked in with flowers and coffee in hand. I spotted her wearing black leggings with a Pocahontas shirt on, so I walked over and gave her a hug as I handed her the coffee and flowers. Then I got down on one knee. As I was holding the ring, I looked up at her in her beautiful brown eyes and said, "Angie Diane Contreras, will you marry me?" She said, "Yes!" and all of the sudden everybody in the restaurant started clapping and cheering. Her friend Trina was working that day. She came running around the corner when she heard all the applause. I attempted to put the ring on her finger, but it was too small. I apologized for that as I went to join everyone else for breakfast.

I came to find out later that she would have preferred for me to propose to her in just about ANY other way. I was a little surprised by that, so I asked why. She explained that she was wearing leggings and a t-shirt and was a hot mess from working while I was dressed up looking and smelling nice. I tried to reason with her that it was a picture of the gospel. You know, Christ comes to His Bride adorned in His flawless garment and divine splendor, while she is dressed in filthy garments. She wasn't buying it. We planned to have the wedding ceremony 3 months later.

Blessed Covenant

The day had finally arrived, February 28th, 2015. I was at the church getting dressed with my 3 groomsmen: Deonte Cary, who was a good friend from the Fire Department; Sean Lewis, who was my best friend; and last but not least, my dad, Maher Ahmed, who was my best man. I was so glad to have my dad, not only at my wedding but in my wedding! After we were all dressed, we prayed with my pastor, who was officiating the wedding. We used the small chapel, which held about 100-125 people. It was packed!

I was standing at the front with my pastor and all my groomsmen by my side. As I heard the music begin to play, I lost it. I started bawling my eyes out. I saw my beautiful bride walking down the aisle. Since she hadn't spoken to her dad in over 10 years, it was very moving to see her escorted by her brother, Bruce. This was the most special day of my life, apart from my salvation. The whole ceremony was perfect! We both shared our testimonies and had Ephesians 2:1-10 read and preached.[2] A bunch of Angie's family and friends were there as she was the only Christian out of them all.

Honeymoon Trip

After we got married, we had a little honeymoon in the Smoky Mountains in North Carolina. We got a cabin in the woods for a few days. We hiked the Smoky Mountains and enjoyed the small, quaint town. After a few days there we headed to the Creation Museum in Kentucky for a couple of days. It was such an amazing time with my beautiful bride, Angie. I couldn't believe it. After everything that had happened during my first marriage, I didn't think I was ever going to get married again.

The first few months of our marriage were wonderful, as you would imagine. We were both working and just enjoying life together. We were members at Colonial Baptist Church in Virginia Beach where my wife ran the coffee bar located in the seminary building. We were reading the Bible and praying together every day as a couple. She also would ask me to pray for us every night in bed before we went to sleep. By God's grace, I not only led her to the Lord, but I was also given the privilege of discipling her as well. This was now God's daughter, and He had entrusted her to me. There is no higher calling than to be covenanted in marriage to one of God's precious daughters.

---

2. Ephesians 2:1–10 (NKJV).

Complementarianism's Opposites

Angie and I had both come from very different backgrounds with different experiences when it came to marriage. I was exposed more to a model where the husband was basically the master of the house, and his wife was his servant. The husband provided the income and ruled with an iron fist. The wife did whatever she was told without question. This sort of belief is very common in Islamic countries. The women over there are NOT equal with men in any way shape or form. They are considered less than men. In some places they are not allowed to vote, drive, get educated etc. They must cover up their entire bodies with a burka in public with just their eyes showing. The men dominate and the women must submit. You are even allowed to beat your wife in Islam as long as it is with a stick that is no bigger in diameter than your pinky.

My wife grew up in the other ditch with more of a feminist mindset. Kind of like the woman who go around saying, "I don't need no man." Or like that saying goes, "Anything he can do I can do better." She was VERY independent and used to running the show. It was the equivalent of woman being the head of the household. Like the curse God placed on Eve in Genesis 3:16 which says, "YOUR DESIRE SHALL BE FOR YOUR HUSBAND, and he shall rule over you."[3] Women by nature want to rule over their husband. These two extreme views of the relationship between a man and a woman in marriage bring to mind two different witnessing encounters.

The first one was on the boardwalk with my sister. She and I were passing out tracts and giving out cold waters. These two Muslim men with their wives were coming our way. The men were walking in the front while their wives were walking behind them covered up wearing their hijabs. I gave them both some tracts and waters and asked where they were from. They were from the Middle East. We had a good conversation. I was able to share the Law and the Gospel with them both. I gave them each a book to read which they willingly accepted. The whole time the women stood behind them without saying a word or even making eye contact if memory serves me well. As we were saying our goodbyes I shook both of their hands. My sister at that point reached out her hand to try and shake theirs as well when the one man said, "I am sorry. It is not right for me to touch another woman's hand who is not my wife. This is what my religion teaches." While my father

3. Genesis 3:16 (NKJV).

was not as extreme as these men, this seemed normal to me. A good movie that captures the essence of this is called *Not Without My Daughter*.[4]

The other encounter was at a Mosque with my father that left me scratching my head. We headed up there together to talk with some of the men about Islam and Christianity. As soon as we arrived, I met a man around my dad's age. He knew I was a Christian and asked why. It always seems to pique people's interest when they hear that my father is a Muslim and I am a Christian, especially other Muslims. So, I was able to share my testimony with him.

My dad then took me over to meet a few other men and introduced me. One of them was an older man who they referred to as the General. He was a General in the military back in his country. He could not speak English that well, so other men were interpreting for both of us. As I was asking questions and interacting with the men all of the sudden about 12-15 women came walking out of their class towards us. They were not your typical Islamic women. They were definitely feminist and mostly American. Instead of the men talking with me, now the lady who was teaching the other women started interacting with me. I was not expecting this.

I tried to ask a question about Jesus dying on the cross, specifically about the verses in the Quran in Surah An-Nisa 4:157-158.[5] As I was trying to articulate my question I got cut off by the lady leading the group. She would say a chapter and verse of the Quran and as she did that all the other women would start reciting it loudly in unison. This went on for a few minutes. The women just kept reciting the Quran to me in Arabic. I was thinking, "What is going on right now?" I did not want to be rude and try to interrupt or talk over them, so I kept quiet.

Eventually my dad spoke up and said, "Please let my son say something." This encounter was the opposite of what I typically had with Muslims. These women were loud and abrasive, basically feminists who put on a hijab and memorized some of the Quran.

Marriage Roles Defined

With all that being said, my wife and I needed a lot of sanctification in the roles we each had in our marriage. My wife early on in our marriage was

4. *Not Without My Daughter*, directed by Brian Gilbert (Metro-Goldwyn-Mayer, 1991), motion picture.

5. Qur'an, Surah An-Nisa 4:157–158.

used to dressing in certain ways which drew more attention to her body than her face. She wasn't the only one. I was guilty of that as well. Over the years the Lord has been so kind in giving her and I a greater desire to dress modestly and with dignity. As I recall Paul Washer saying in a sermon, quoting his wife Charo, "If your clothing is a frame for your face, from which the glory of God is to shine, it's proper, if it draws attention to your face. If your clothing draws attention to your body, to outline it, to make it noticed, then it's sensual and God hates it."

So now that we were married, we learned that the Bible teaches something drastically different than what either one of us were exposed to. Men and women are equal in value and worth and at the same time have different roles. There are some things men can do that women can't and vice versa. Women can have babies whereas men can't, and men can preach where women can't according to the Apostle Paul. Sadly, some professing Christians take issue with what I just said, but that doesn't surprise me at all. Those who cannot endure sound doctrine love to have their ears itched.

The roles for the husbands and wives are clearly laid out in Scripture. Knowing what those roles are is not the hard part, it is the doing of those roles that we have trouble with. Ephesians 5:22-27 says, "Wives, submit to your own husbands, as to the Lord. For the husband is head of the wife, as also Christ is head of the church; and He is the Savior of the body. Therefore, just as the church is subject to Christ, so let the wives be to their own husbands in everything. Husbands, love your wives, just as Christ also loved the church and gave Himself for her, that He might sanctify and cleanse her with the washing of water by the word, that He might present her to Himself a glorious church, not having spot or wrinkle or any such thing, but that she should be holy and without blemish."[6]

My role is to love my wife as Christ loved the Church. How did Christ love His bride? He prayed for His bride (John 17:6-26). He rebuked His bride (Matthew 16:21-23). He protected His bride from false teaching (Matthew 16:5-12). He protected His bride physically (John 18:1-9). He served His bride (Matthew 20:25-28). He provided for His bride financially (Matthew 17:24-27). He fed His bride (John 21:9-12). He provided clothing for His bride (Isaiah 61:10). He ultimately laid down His life for His bride (John 10:11). 1 Corinthians 16:13 says, "Be on the alert, stand

6. Ephesians 5:22–27 (NKJV).

firm in the faith, ACT LIKE MEN, be strong."[7] How do we as husbands act like men? By looking to Christ in His word as the Spirit empowers us to be more and more like Him.

The wife's role is laid out in Titus 2 as well as other places in Scripture. Titus 2:3-5 says, "The older women likewise, that they be reverent in behavior, not slanderers, not given to much wine, teachers of good things—that they admonish the young women to love their husbands, to love their children, to be discreet, chaste, homemakers, good, obedient to their own husbands, that the word of God may not be blasphemed."[8]

Why are these roles so important? The end of verse 5 tells us, so "that the word of God may not be blasphemed." This is what marriage is all about! Glorifying God by obeying Him so that He is praised and not blasphemed. Marriage is a picture of the Gospel. I am so thankful to God for my wife. She has grown in so many ways and it has been so encouraging to have a front row view of it all.

Gift of a Daughter

Angie is my best friend. I love her so much and am so thankful to the Lord for her. God has given me one of His precious daughters to love and cherish. We banter back and forth, all the time, about who loves who more, and I ALWAYS win. Why? Because Scripture says, "She loved MUCH because she has been forgiven MUCH!" I WIN! I have been forgiven MUCH! God has forgiven me for so much and so has my wife. I have found a good thing, Angie. "He who finds a wife finds a good thing and obtains favor from the LORD."[9] I am the most unworthy, undeserving person I know, and God continues to pour out His grace upon me.

I will never forget something I learned from a preacher once. Whenever he would fly on a plane, he would usually get into a conversation with the person he sat next to. They would always end up asking him, "What do you do for a living?"

I loved his response: "I am a husband."

Then they would say, "No, like, what else do you do?"

---

7. 1 Corinthians 16:13 (NKJV); cf. John 17:6–26; Matthew 16:21–23; Matthew 16:5–12; John 18:1–9; Matthew 20:25–28; John 10:11.

8. Titus 2:3–5 (NKJV).

9. Matthew Henry, *Commentary on the Whole Bible* (Grand Rapids, MI: Zondervan, 1960), s.v. Genesis 2:21–25.

He would respond with, "I am a father." The point he was making is very important. His first ministry was his wife, and his second was his children. That is what I hope to model. My wife is my first ministry, and then my children. God has given a wretch like me His precious daughter to love and care for. Is that fair? NO, it is GRACE!

We have now been married for ten years as I write this. We are in our early 40s, and I pray God gives us many more years together here on earth! Whether He does or doesn't, I still get to spend eternity with my bride and sister worshiping our Lord TOGETHER forever! It doesn't get any better than that! Matthew Henry said it best, speaking of Eve, "She was not made out of his head to rule over him, nor out of his feet to be trampled upon by him, but out of his side to be equal with him, under his arm to be protected, and near his heart to be beloved."[10]

"Now to Him who is able to do exceedingly abundantly above all that we ask or think, according to the power that works in us, to Him be glory in the church by Christ Jesus to all generations, forever and ever. Amen." Ephesians 3:20,21[11]

10. Proverbs 19:14 (NKJV).

11. Ephesians 3:20–21 (NKJV).

Before the Throne of God Above

Words by Charitie Lees Bancroft, 1863

Before the throne of God above
I have a strong and perfect plea,
A great High Priest whose name is Love,
Who ever lives and pleads for me.
My name is graven on His hands,
My name is written on His heart;
I know that while in heav'n He stands
No tongue can bid me thence depart,
No tongue can bid me thence depart.

When Satan tempts me to despair
And tells me of the guilt within,
Upward I look and see Him there
Who made an end of all my sin.
Because the sinless Savior died
My sinful soul is counted free;
For God the Just is satisfied
To look on Him and pardon me,
To look on Him and pardon me.

Behold Him there! The risen Lamb,
My perfect, spotless righteousness;
The great unchangeable "I AM,"
The King of glory and of grace!
One with Himself I cannot die,
My soul is purchased by His blood;
My life is hid with Christ on high,
With Christ, my Savior and my God,
With Christ, my Savior and my God![12]

---

12. Charitie Lees Bancroft, "Before the Throne of God Above," in *The Hymnal for Worship and Celebration* (Waco, TX: Word Music, 1986), hymn no. 231.

Chapter 6

What's in a Name?

"Behold, children are a heritage from the Lord, the fruit of the womb is a reward. Like arrows in the hand of a warrior, so are the children of one's youth. Happy is the man who has his quiver full of them; They shall not be ashamed, but shall speak with their enemies in the gate." Psalm 127:3-5[1]

A Father's Joy

THE YEAR WAS 2018, and I was at Texas Roadhouse with my beautiful bride, enjoying some of the best food on the planet. We were having a nice steak dinner together. During our meal, my wife pulls out this gift bag with a card and hands it to me. I was wondering to myself, "What is this all about?" So, I began to read the card and realized that I am now a father! My wife surprised me with the best news ever at my favorite restaurant. That is how you do it, ladies. I didn't actually tear up until I went to see the ultrasound, where I first saw my daughter moving around in her mother's womb. That is when it really hit me. . . I am a father now! I was thinking, "Lord, not only did you save a wretch like me and give me one of your daughters to love and cherish, but now you have entrusted me with a precious little baby girl. You

---

1. Psalm 127:3-5 (New King James Version).

are so kind!" Angie found a special way to surprise me with her other two pregnancies as well. The surprises got better every single time.

I was blessed to have learned sound doctrine from the moment of my conversion. Early on in my walk with the Lord, I remember hearing Christians talk about something called the "Doctrines of Grace." As they explained what they were, I remember saying to myself, "Sounds good to me. That's what the Bible teaches." I am a Bible guy. If you can show me where the Bible teaches something, I will believe it. What I didn't know was how controversial they were. In the year 2016, I found out in an unexpected way.

Theology Matters

I used to be a big Mark Cahill supporter. I met him when I went to a Deeper Conference, where he was one of the speakers along with Ray Comfort in 2008. He wrote one of the best books on evangelism called *One Thing You Can't Do in Heaven*.[2] The one thing you can't do in heaven is witness to lost people because there will be none there. He also wrote another great book called *One Heartbeat Away* for lost people.[3] I used to buy both of those books in bulk to give out to everyone I talked to. If they were a Christian, they got *One Thing You Can't Do in Heaven*, and if they were an unbeliever, they got the other one. It was awesome!

In 2016, I placed a big order of books from his ministry. I sent him an email asking if he was planning on going to the atheist reason rally with the Living Waters guys for some witnessing. His response was not what I had expected.

He said, "Nope. I don't go witnessing with those guys anymore. They teach a false doctrine called Calvinism." I was really confused. At this point in my life, I knew the differences between a Calvinist and an Arminian. I knew Christian men have differed on this for years but still considered each other brothers and friends. One example was George Whitefield and John Wesley.[4]

2. Mark Cahill, One Thing You Can't Do in Heaven (Rockwall, TX: Biblical Discipleship Ministries, 2004).

3. Mark Cahill, One Heartbeat Away: Your Journey into Eternity (Rockwall, TX: Biblical Discipleship Ministries, 2005).

4. Arnold A. Dallimore, George Whitefield: The Life and Times of the Great Evangelist of the Eighteenth-Century Revival (Carlisle, PA: Banner of Truth, 1970), 1:497–500.

In Mark Cahill's book, *One Thing You Can't Do in Heaven*, at the beginning of each chapter, he would have a quote from, guess who? Charles Spurgeon. . . Spurgeon was a Calvinist! Spurgeon is known for saying, "Calvinism is the gospel, and nothing else."[5] So, I wrote him back and asked him why he couldn't partner with Living Waters in the area of evangelism seeing that one of his books is full of quotes by the Calvinist Charles Spurgeon. I also reminded him of the friendship between George Whitefield and John Wesley. I asked him why he sells books that have quotes by Charles Spurgeon at the beginning of every chapter if he believes Calvinism is a false teaching. He never emailed me back, so I stopped buying his books. I was very disappointed.

Tulip and Her Points

After we were married, my wife and I would have a time of worship together every day. I actually think we started doing it before we were married, but over the phone. Early on in our marriage, I remember us sitting down one day to pray and read together for family worship. It was then I explained to her the doctrines of grace. We went from passage after passage to see where the Bible teaches these beautiful truths. They are also known by the acronym TULIP. The T stands for Total Depravity, which simply means man, in his fallen nature, hates God and is completely unable to do anything to save himself because his entire nature (body, will, mind, emotions, etc.) has been corrupted by sin.[6] The U stands for Unconditional Election, which means God chose to save some before the creation, not based on anything at all in the elect persons, but according to His sovereign good pleasure and eternal purpose.[7] The L stands for Limited Atonement. This doctrine teaches that Christ died ONLY for His people. Every person who would ever repent and believe in Christ are the ONLY ones He died for.[8] The I stands for Irresistible Grace, which means when God saves a person, He changes their nature so they will not resist coming to Him. Instead of hating God and running from Him in rebellion, His grace changes them,

5. Charles H. Spurgeon, "A Defense of Calvinism," in The New Park Street Pulpit Sermons, vol. 4 (London: Passmore & Alabaster, 1858), 337.

6. Romans 3:10-18 (New King James Version).

7. Ephesians 1:4-5 (New King James Version).

8. John 10:11, 15 (New King James Version).

so they willingly repent and believe in Christ.[9] The P stands for Perseverance or Preservation of the Saints. This means that all who Christ saves will persevere to the end. He will lose NONE![10]

These doctrines are so comforting to the Christian. They are humbling and give the believer great assurance! They give God the maximum amount of glory most of all. My wife believed these doctrines as well. Therefore, we decided to name our daughter Tulip. Her name has been a great conversation starter and has provided many witnessing opportunities already. My grandma from Egypt, who I call Teta, was named Sameha. It is an old-fashioned name that means ongoing forgiveness. What a perfect middle name to have paired with Tulip. I wanted to honor her and show her how much we loved her, so we decided to name our daughter Tulip Sameha Ahmed.

London's Great Confession

The first Christian conference we went to together was called the G3 Conference, held in Atlanta, Georgia, in 2017. We have been going every year since, and it is one of our favorites! By this time, I had grown quite a bit in my knowledge and understanding of Christ due to the many godly men I would listen to online. One of those godly men was Dr. James White of Alpha and Omega Ministries. I listened to Dr. White on The Dividing Line all the time and still do. The thing that really struck me about him was how much respect he showed for his opponents. What I mean by that is he would never strawman them. He would always accurately represent their position. That spoke volumes to me. I mean, if you have the truth, there is no need to lie about the opposing view. Truth can defend itself, plus lying is a sin. So, as I listened to him on his program, I would hear him mention something called the Second London Baptist Confession. He said he was a Reformed Baptist and that was the confession he held to.[11]

Dr. James White is one of my favorite teachers and debaters. I have benefited greatly from his ministry. So, after hearing him say he holds to the Second London Baptist Confession, as well as others like Voddie Baucham and Paul Washer, I decided to pick it up and read through it myself. I was blown away! I was like, why didn't anybody share this with me after I became

9. John 6:44 (New King James Version).

10. John 10:28-29 (New King James Version).

11. Second London Baptist Confession of Faith (1689), in A Faith to Confess: The Baptist Confession of Faith of 1689 (Leeds: Carey Publications, 1975).

a Christian? It would have been so helpful in teaching me what the Bible says in a concise way. I already believed most everything contained in it. So, after reading it and sharing it with my wife, I said, "I guess I am a Reformed Baptist," and we adopted the confession for ourselves. 1689 for life!

I share all that to say, when my wife got pregnant with our second child, I knew immediately what I wanted to name him or her: LONDON! This child would be our SECOND child, and we loved the SECOND LONDON Baptist Confession, so it made perfect sense. I was willing to name the child London whether it was a boy or a girl, but in God's kind providence, He gave us a little boy. So, his first name was London! He still needed a middle name, and I had that in mind as well. I was saved by hearing Ray Comfort share the gospel with people on his television show called The Way of the Master in 2006.[12] In honor of Ray Comfort, we decided to name him London Comfort Ahmed. Ray Comfort will always have a very special place in my heart. God saved me through his ministry. I pray and hope that London will reflect the name we have given him one day. To be an evangelist like Ray Comfort while holding to the Second London Baptist Confession would make this Baba so happy!

Judah, I Don't Know Why You're Clapping

The last time my wife got pregnant was so exciting. We both had been praying again for another child. The Lord answered our prayer in the affirmative once more. It was still difficult for my wife because she was in her 40s and considered high risk. Regardless, we were over the moon with God's excessive kindness toward us. It was time again to think of names for the coming baby boy. Two names came to mind immediately. Being Egyptian, I liked the name Zaphnath-Paaneah, which was Joseph's Egyptian name given to him by Pharaoh.[13] The other one was Athanasius. He was a Bishop of Alexandria in Egypt who defended the deity of Christ against the Arian heresy. He was given the nickname Athanasius Contra Mundum, which means Athanasius against the world.[14] Pretty awesome

---

12. Ray Comfort, The Way of the Master (Lake Forest, CA: Living Waters Publications, 2006), television program.

13. Genesis 41:45 (New King James Version).

14. Athanasius, On the Incarnation, trans. John Behr (Yonkers, NY: St. Vladimir's Seminary Press, 2011), 9–12.

names, right!? My wife didn't think so. She said, "No!" Can you believe the nerve of her? Well, it was worth a try.

I once heard Voddie Baucham preach a great sermon about Joseph in the book of Genesis.[15] It is a well-known story in the Bible. I have usually heard it preached in a way that focus's in on his hardships, suffering, and how God raised him up to second in power, etc. The main point always seemed to be on Joseph and how you can dare to be a Joseph, or something like that. Voddie preached it differently. The central theme for the book of Genesis is found in Genesis 3:15 which says, "And I will put enmity between you and the woman, and between your seed and her Seed; He shall bruise your head, and you shall bruise His heel."[16] This is referred to as the Proto-evangelium, which means first gospel. I would argue that this is the central theme for the whole Bible. The Bible is about the Seed of the woman who will crush the head of the serpent. As you read through the Bible, starting in Genesis, you should say to yourself, "Is this the promised Seed? Nope, he sinned. Maybe this is the one? Nope, he sinned." So, the story of Joseph is not really about Joseph; it is ultimately about Jesus! The story of Joseph being sold into slavery is a story about God preserving Judah, so that, the Lion from the tribe of Judah, JESUS, could come one day and crush the head of the serpent! Genesis 49:10 says, "The scepter shall not depart from Judah, nor a lawgiver from between his feet, until Shiloh comes; And to Him shall be the obedience of the people."[17] This is why I love the name Judah so much! Our Lord and Savior comes from the tribe of Judah!

Another favorite preacher of mine is Paul David Washer. He has had the biggest impact on my life besides Ray Comfort. He was a missionary in Peru for 10 years and founded the HeartCry Missionary Society, which supports indigenous missionaries.[18] I have never met a man who preached with as much passion and zeal as Brother Washer does. I remember watching a sermon by him called "Shocking Youth Message" years ago. It was the best sermon I have ever heard![19] My two mentors of

15. Voddie Baucham, "The Gospel According to Joseph," sermon, Grace Family Baptist Church, Spring, TX, January 15, 2012, https://www.sermonaudio.com/sermoninfo.asp?SID=1151215343510.

16. Genesis 3:15 (New King James Version).

17. Genesis 49:10 (New King James Version).

18. Paul Washer, "About HeartCry," HeartCry Missionary Society, accessed April 19, 2025, https://heartcrymissionary.com/about/.

19. Paul Washer, "Shocking Youth Message," sermon, Montgomery, AL, 2002, https://www.youtube.com/watch?v=uuabITeO4ho.

the faith would have to be Ray Comfort and Paul Washer. I refer to them as the "Sons of Thunder!"[20] I have learned so much from both of these men. For these reasons, we decided to name our last child Judah Washer Ahmed! May God not only save Judah but raise him up to be a missionary and preach like Brother Paul Washer!

Sharpening Arrows

Our greatest desire and prayer for our children is for them to know the Lord. We know God uses means to answer prayer. One of those means, we love to enjoy together as a family, is Family Worship. I look forward to it more than anything else in my day. As a family with three little ones, we have a time of worship almost every day. It can be challenging at times with a 6-year-old, 4-year-old, and 1-year-old, but by God's grace, we do it. We typically open with prayer, sing a song, read a short section of Scripture, ask some questions from the Baptist Catechism,[21] memorize some verses from the Bible, sing the law and gospel in a jingle, finish with the doxology, and close in prayer. My wife created the jingle, and here's how it goes: "We broke God's Law; Jesus paid it all. The Law says do; the Gospel says done!"

Knowing the difference between the Law and the Gospel is essential. Charles Spurgeon once said, "There is no point on which men make greater mistakes than on the relation which exists between the law and the gospel. Some men put the law instead of the gospel; others put gospel instead of the law. A certain class maintains that the law and the gospel are mixed . . . These men understand not the truth and are false teachers."[22] As one preacher often says, "If you can't say Amen, you ought to say ouch!"

"A good man leaves an inheritance to his children's children."[23] That is what we want to do with ours. Of course, we want to leave them a house with land and money, if possible, but we ultimately want to leave them with the gospel! Everything else will be destroyed by moth, rust and fire

20. Mark 3:17 (New King James Version).

21. The Baptist Catechism (1693), in A Faith to Confess: The Baptist Confession of Faith of 1689 (Leeds: Carey Publications, 1975), 75–93.

22. Charles H. Spurgeon, "The Law and the Gospel," in The Metropolitan Tabernacle Pulpit Sermons, vol. 34 (London: Passmore & Alabaster, 1888), 541.

23. Proverbs 13:22 (New King James Version).

but Christ is of infinite value.[24] Matthew 6:33 says, "Seek first the Kingdom of God and His righteousness, and all these things shall be added to you."[25] I also plan on leaving my most valuable item to my daughter Tulip one day, if she will have it. What is that, you might ask? Why, my Evidence Study Bible by Ray Comfort, of course![26] As I like to say, "MY Bible has all the answers." I had a John MacArthur Study Bible when I first became a believer. I read it from cover to cover.[27] Then I upgraded to the Reformation Study Bible by R.C. Sproul. I read every footnote and article in that as well.[28] Then I finally found the cream of the crop. . . The Evidence Study Bible by Ray Comfort! I am so thankful for all 3 of those Study Bibles and would highly recommend them all.

From the Mouth of Babes

In the Bible, names have meaning. All three of our children have names that are very meaningful. Our hope and prayer are for our children to be a living testimony to their names. Here is a sweet example where we have already seen a little glimpse. One of the happiest moments I have had as a father was a couple of years ago when we were eating at a little diner in our town. My daughter Tulip must have been about 3. There was another family eating in the diner with us. We were almost done eating when Tulip said, "Baba (Daddy in Arabic), can we give that family over there a gospel tract?" I was ready to baptize her after I heard her say that! Here is my little girl wanting to tell those around us about Jesus. So, I said, "Of course, Sameha!" We grabbed a booklet, and I held her hand as we walked up to their table. We introduced ourselves, and I said, "My daughter asked me if we could give you guys a Don't Stub Your Toe gospel booklet."[29]

---

24. Matthew 6:19-20 (New King James Version).

25. Matthew 6:33 (New King James Version).

26. Ray Comfort, ed., The Evidence Study Bible (Gainesville, FL: Bridge-Logos, 2011).

27. John MacArthur, ed., The MacArthur Study Bible (Nashville: Thomas Nelson, 1997).

28. R.C. Sproul, ed., The Reformation Study Bible (Orlando: Ligonier Ministries, 2005).

29. Todd Friel, Don't Stub Your Toe (Fortis Institute, 2017), gospel booklet.

They said, "Sure." So, Tulip handed them the booklet. They thanked her, and we asked them to please read it when they have time. Then we paid for our meal, got in our car, prayed for them, and headed home.

Tulip has joined me at festivals, where we set up a booth to share the gospel and pass out tracts. She passed out a lot last year and really enjoyed it. She has a purse she takes with her when we go out, and it is always full of gospel tracts. There is nothing sweeter than seeing your child worship the Lord through evangelism. Jesus said, "Out of the mouth of babes and nursing infants You have perfected praise."[30]

Let There Be Three

With all that being said, we were hoping to have one more child, but the Lord said no. He gave us 3, and that is exactly what we needed. We have a good Father who loves us so much! One of my favorite things about our children is to hear them sing songs about the Lord. Judah can't talk yet but likes to dance when he hears music. Tulip likes to watch the videos that go with the songs. London struggles with his pronunciation of words, but it sounds so cute when he sings! Especially Holy, Holy, Holy. It is one of his favorite songs to sing. It is one of my favorites too. This is just another example of good things happening to bad people. Is it fair? Nope, it is GRACE!

"In the year that King Uzziah died, I saw the Lord sitting on a throne, high and lifted up, and the train of His robe filled the temple. Above it stood seraphim; each one had six wings: with two he covered his face, with two he covered his feet, and with two he flew. And one cried to another and said: 'Holy, holy, holy is the Lord of hosts; The whole earth is full of His glory!'" Isaiah 6:1-3[31]

30. Matthew 21:16 (New King James Version).
31. Isaiah 6:1-3 (New King James Version).

Holy, Holy, Holy! Lord God Almighty!
Words by Reginald Heber, 1827

Holy, holy, holy! Lord God Almighty!
Early in the morning our song shall rise to Thee;
Holy, holy, holy, merciful and mighty!
God in three Persons, blessed Trinity!

Holy, holy, holy! All the saints adore Thee,
Casting down their golden crowns around the glassy sea,
Cherubim and seraphim falling down before Thee,
Who wert and art, and evermore shalt be.

Holy, holy, holy! Though the darkness hide Thee,
Though the eye of sinful man Thy glory may not see;
Only Thou art holy; there is none beside Thee,
Perfect in power, love, and purity.

Holy, holy, holy! Lord God Almighty!
All Thy works shall praise Thy name in earth and sky and sea;
Holy, holy, holy, merciful and mighty!
God in three Persons, blessed Trinity![32]

---

32. Reginald Heber, "Holy, Holy, Holy! Lord God Almighty!," in Hymns, Written and Adapted to the Weekly Church Service of the Year (London: J. Heber, 1827), no. 22.

Chapter 7

The Rod of Love

"As many as I love, I rebuke and chasten. Therefore be zealous and repent." Revelation 3:19[1]

WHEN I WAS IN 5th grade, my sister and I each invited a friend to spend the night. We had a brilliant plan to sneak out of our apartment at midnight. We lived in an apartment complex back then, and when the hour arrived, we stuffed pillows under our blankets and rolled up towels for heads—a foolproof disguise, or so we thought. But my sister was too tired to join us. So, it was just me, Brian, and Brittany, the faithful rebels. We crept out and roamed the complex, exhilarated by the thrill of doing something forbidden. It didn't last long. My parents got up to use the bathroom and noticed three missing kids. They woke my sister, who spilled the beans about our scheme. Furious, they tracked us down, hauled us back, and sent Brian and Brittany to bed. Then came my reckoning. I alone was disciplined. Why not my friends? They disobeyed too, didn't they? Simple: they weren't my parents' children. You ONLY discipline your own.

My life passage isn't one I would have picked—but it suits me very well. It's Hebrews 12:3-11: "For consider Him who endured such hostility from sinners against Himself, lest you become weary and discouraged in your souls. You have not yet resisted to bloodshed, striving against sin. And you have forgotten the exhortation which speaks to you as to sons: 'My son, do not despise the chastening of the Lord, nor be discouraged when you are

1. Revelation 3:19 (New King James Version).

THE ROD OF LOVE

rebuked by Him; for whom the Lord loves He chastens, and scourges every son whom He receives.' If you endure chastening, God deals with you as with sons; for what son is there whom a father does not chasten? But if you are without chastening, of which all have become partakers, then you are illegitimate and not sons. Furthermore, we have had human fathers who corrected us, and we paid them respect. Shall we not much more readily be in subjection to the Father of spirits and live? For they indeed for a few days chastened us as seemed best to them, but He for our profit, that we may be partakers of His holiness. Now no chastening seems to be joyful for the present, but painful; nevertheless, afterward it yields the peaceable fruit of righteousness to those who have been trained by it."[2] This passage is so precious to me now. It's about the Father's love expressed through discipline.

The Gift No One Wants

I find it curious that there are many promises in the Bible Christians never claim as their life verses. One example would be 2 Timothy 3:12, "Yes, and all who desire to live godly in Christ Jesus will suffer persecution."[3] Or Philippians 1:29, "For to you it has been granted on behalf of Christ, not only to believe in Him, but also to suffer for His sake."[4] The last thing any of us wants is to suffer or be persecuted. But when you actually read the Bible, you not only see it as something good, but by God's grace, you will also rejoice, like the Apostles, when it happens. "So they departed from the presence of the council, rejoicing that they were counted worthy to suffer shame for His name."[5] Peter in his epistle also encouraged believers to rejoice when they suffered. "But rejoice to the extent that you partake of Christ's sufferings, that when His glory is revealed, you may also be glad with exceeding joy."[6] Many Christians today desire comfortable and pain-free lives, myself included, but our great Father in heaven loves us too much for that. He desires something far better.

My story reflects this truth: good things (like discipline) happen to bad people (like me) because I'm a child of God. Many Christians have "life verses" they claim, frequently misapplied. Take Jeremiah 29:11: "For

2. Hebrews 12:3-11 (New King James Version).

3. 2 Timothy 3:12 (New King James Version).

4. Philippians 1:29 (New King James Version).

5. Acts 5:41 (New King James Version).

6. 1 Peter 4:13 (New King James Version).

I know the plans I have for you," declares the Lord, "plans to prosper you and not to harm you, plans to give you hope and a future."[7] Or Philippians 4:13, "I can do all things through Christ who strengthens me."[8] This means I can win the UFC championship, right? I don't think so. Paul was in prison when he wrote that and knew what it was to be hungry and to be full, to abound and to suffer. He was saying he can ENDURE all things through Christ who gives him strength. When I hear people quote these verses and twist them, as they so often do, I hear Paul Washer's voice in my head saying, "Twist not Scripture lest ye be like Satan."[9]

The Beauty of Adoption

If anything can bring out the old Galal, it is when people say, "We are ALL children of God." I really think I hear a hissing sound every time those words are uttered. Scripture could not be more emphatic about this: by nature, we are "children of wrath" (Ephesians 2:3), "sons of disobedience" (Colossians 3:6), and our "father is the devil" (John 8:44).[10] "That is, it is not the children of the flesh who are children of God, but the children of the promise are regarded as descendants."[11] The doctrine of adoption is one of the most stunning truths in all of Scripture. Galatians 4:4-5 says, "But when the fullness of the time had come, God sent forth His Son, born of a woman, born under the law, to redeem those who were under the law, that we might receive the adoption as sons."[12] John 1:12 states, "But as many as received Him, to them He gave the right to *become* children of God, to those who believe in His name."[13] We become His children through faith in Christ. God justifies us, *adopts* us, and sanctifies (positionally) us at the moment of conversion. If you don't understand this foundational truth, then you will never understand the beauty of the gospel.

7. Jeremiah 29:11 (New King James Version).

8. Philippians 4:13 (New King James Version).

9. Ray Comfort, ed., *The Evidence Study Bible* (Gainesville, FL: Bridge-Logos, 2011), s.v. "Twist not Scripture lest ye be like Satan."

10. Ephesians 2:3; Colossians 3:6; John 8:44 (New King James Version).

11. Romans 9:8 (New King James Version).

12. Galatians 4:4-5 (New King James Version).

13. John 1:12 (New King James Version).

The Second London Baptist Confession says this in chapter 12 on adoption: "God has vouchsafed, that in Christ, His only Son, and for His sake, all those who are justified shall be made partakers of the grace of adoption, by which they are taken into the number of the children of God and enjoy their liberties and privileges. They have His name put upon them, and receive the Spirit of adoption. They have access to the throne of grace with boldness, and are enabled to cry, 'Abba, Father!' They are pitied, protected, provided for, and chastened by Him as by a father, yet they are never cast off, but are sealed to the day of redemption, when they inherit the promises as heirs of everlasting salvation."[14]

Love Can't Stay Silent

One hot summer, a group of us headed to a Pride Festival in Norfolk, Virginia, ready to share the gospel. This was a pretty big festival that was praising the LGBTQ+ folks. We arrived armed with coolers brimming with water and stacks of books to distribute. The book, *Audacity*, penned by Julia Zwayne and Ray Comfort, was essentially the video of the same name in written form—a powerful piece from Living Waters tackling homosexuality and marriage.[15] That place felt like one of the darkest I'd ever evangelized, yet the darker the setting, the brighter the gospel shined forth. It reminded me of when our Savior came into the world, "the light shines in the darkness, and the darkness did not overcome it."[16]

As we were passing out books and waters, I saw two girls walking my way, holding hands. As they got closer, I said, "Did y'all get one of these? It's a free book."

One of them reached out and took it. As she grabbed it from me, I asked if they would like a free water to go with it. They stopped and said, "Yes, please. Thank you." So, I opened up my cooler and grabbed two bottles of water. As I handed them the waters, I asked if they were here for the festival.

14. Second London Baptist Confession of Faith (1689), chap. 12, in A Faith to Confess: The Baptist Confession of Faith of 1689 (Leeds: Carey Publications, 1975), 25.

15. Julia Zwayne and Ray Comfort, Audacity: Love Can't Stay Silent (Alachua, FL: Bridge-Logos, 2016).

16. John 1:5 (New King James Version).

They said, "Yes, we are." They were excited for such an event to support their lifestyle. I found out that one was in the Navy, and they were planning on getting "married" soon.

I remember thinking to myself, "This could go not so well." After getting to know them a little bit, I asked them what they believed about the afterlife. They believed in heaven and hell. I then asked if they would consider themselves to be a good person, and if they would make it to heaven.

They said, "Yes." So, I opened up the Law and we started going through the Commandments. As I was in the middle of asking them a question, an older lady came up to us and rudely interrupted.

She said to the girls, "Is this guy bothering you?!"

The girls looked at her with a look of bewilderment and said, "No. We are just talking."

The older lady said, "Okay, just don't let him push his hate on you," as she walked away. Come to find out, the older lady was a professing Christian. She was there hating these people by telling them lies that they were God's children and how He loves them and accepts them just as they are.

After she walked away, the girls looked back at me, and I said, "Am I bothering you? Am I pushing any hate on y'all?"

They said, "No, we wouldn't have stopped if we didn't want to talk."

After we went through the commandments, the girls realized they were condemned by the Law despite their lesbianism. In fact, up to this point, I didn't even mention it. Their mouths were stopped, and they were ready for the good news of the gospel. After sharing the gospel with them, I told them that God commands all men (and women) everywhere to repent and believe in the gospel.[17]

I said, "That means you agree with God about your sin and turn your back on it in every way as you place your trust in Christ alone." I told them they must repent of ALL their sin, which included their lesbianism and their desire to be "married" to each other, which is only between a man and a woman.[18] The young lady in the Navy was very eager to listen as I was sharing this with her, but her girlfriend was becoming more uncomfortable.

The Navy gal then asked me a question. She said, "Why is my wanting to be married to my girlfriend sinful? I was born this way, so God must be okay with it, right?"

17. Acts 17:30 (New King James Version).
18. Genesis 2:24; Matthew 19:4-6 (New King James Version).

I said, "That is a great question. The answer is simple. It is not okay because God says it is sinful. 1 Corinthians 6:9-11 says, 'Do you not know that the unrighteous will not inherit the kingdom of God? Do not be deceived. Neither fornicators, nor idolaters, nor adulterers, nor homosexuals, nor sodomites, nor thieves, nor covetous, nor drunkards, nor revilers, nor extortioners will inherit the kingdom of God. And such were some of you. But you were washed, but you were sanctified, but you were justified in the name of the Lord Jesus and by the Spirit of our God.' Jesus told Nicodemus in John 3 that 'You must be born again.'"[19] I explained to them that we are ALL born with a sinful nature. That is why Jesus said we must be born again. We cannot enter the kingdom of God unless we are born from above. The moment we repent and trust in Christ alone is when conversion happens. That is when we are adopted by God and become His son or daughter. We go from being children of wrath to children of God. That is the good news of the gospel! I thanked them for stopping and having the conversation. I gave them a copy of Audacity on DVD and asked them to please watch it and give this some serious thought.[20]

The Navy girl said, "We will watch it tonight in our hotel room." She gave me a hug and said, "Thank you for the conversation and the way you talked with us." I prayed for them both as they headed into the festival.

Painful Chastening

After God adopted me, my life has been one of chastening. The Lord has not let me go my own way; He loves me too much for that! He has come time and time again with His rod of love. After becoming a Christian, I wish I could say I stopped sinning, but honestly, that hasn't been the case. Before I was a Christian, I never gave a thought to fighting sin. I ONLY loved it and indulged in it as I pleased. After becoming a Christian, the war began. Paul captures this truth in Romans 7:21-23, "I find then a law, that evil is present with me, the one who wills to do good. For I delight in the law of God according to the inward man. But I see another law in my members, warring against the law of my mind, and bringing me into captivity to the law of sin which is in my members."[21]

19. 1 Corinthians 6:9-11; John 3:3 (New King James Version).
20. Audacity, directed by Ray Comfort (Santa Clarita, CA: Living Waters Publications, 2015), DVD.
21. Romans 7:21-23 (New King James Version).

Early on in our marriage, I made a profile on a dating app. A brother from church found out and confronted me about it over lunch. By God's grace, I repented and confessed my sin to our pastor and to my wife. That was not enjoyable at all, but it did ultimately bring about the peaceable fruit of righteousness. God loved me so much that He used a brother to rebuke me for my sin. After that, we began biblical counseling, ACBC (Association of Certified Biblical Counselors).[22] It was super helpful. I have had many times in my life where God has come to me with the rod through a brother, or a sermon, or just driving down the road, or reading my Bible. I am so glad He loves me. Romans 9:13 says, "Jacob I have loved, but Esau I have hated."[23] Paul Washer once said about Jacob and Esau, "How is it that God's hatred was manifested toward Esau? God never disciplined Esau; He let Esau be Esau. But He loved Jacob by beating the living daylights out of him all his life."[24]

Sexual sin has been a besetting sin for me before and after my marriage. I would look at pornography for a time, then, as I would listen to a sermon, God the Holy Spirit would convict me of my sin. I remember once going for a jog in my neighborhood while listening to a sermon by Paul Washer on the holiness of God.[25] I literally stopped in the middle of my run, convicted of my sin, and cried out to God in tears. If you ever want to be convicted of sin, listen to Paul Washer. It never fails. Godly sorrow is a wonderful gift from the Lord that leads to repentance. "For observe this very thing, that you sorrowed in a godly manner: What diligence it produced in you, what clearing of yourselves, what indignation, what fear, what vehement desire, what zeal, what vindication! In all things you proved yourselves to be clear in this matter."[26] The beautiful thing about being convicted of sin for the believer is we have a throne of grace to run to. "Let us therefore come boldly to the throne of grace, that we may obtain mercy and find grace to help in time of need."[27]

22. Association of Certified Biblical Counselors, "About ACBC," accessed April 19, 2025, https://biblicalcounseling.com/about/.

23. Romans 9:13 (New King James Version).

24. Paul Washer, "Jacob I Loved, Esau I Hated," sermon, Grace Community Church, Huntsville, AL, March 12, 2017, https://www.sermonaudio.com/sermoninfo.asp?SID=313171135351.

25. Paul Washer, "The Holiness of God," sermon, HeartCry Missionary Conference, 2015, https://www.youtube.com/watch?v=oQol6LT2Yoo.

26. 2 Corinthians 7:10-11 (New King James Version).

27. Hebrews 4:16 (New King James Version).

I have had seasons of sin in my life, which have caused me to doubt my salvation. But by God's grace, He has always come for me and worked repentance in my heart, restoring the JOY of my salvation.[28] The Second London Baptist Confession is helpful regarding this. The chapter on "Perseverance of the Saints," paragraph 3, says, "They may fall into grievous sins and continue in them for a time, due to the temptation of Satan and the world, the strength of corruption remaining in them, and the neglect of means of their preservation. In so doing, they incur God's displeasure and grieve His Holy Spirit; their graces and comforts become impaired; their hearts are hardened and their consciences wounded; they hurt and scandalize others and bring temporary judgments on themselves. Nevertheless, they will renew their repentance and be preserved through faith in Christ Jesus to the end."[29]

Peaceable Fruit of Righteousness

My marriage has been a picture of God coming time and time again with correction. I have sinned against my wife repeatedly, and yet she has continued to forgive me time and time again. Is that fair? No, it is grace! She has demonstrated forgiveness on a level I've never witnessed in anyone else. Luke 17:3-4 says, "Take heed to yourselves. If your brother sins against you, rebuke him; and if he repents, forgive him. And if he sins against you seven times in a day, and seven times in a day returns to you saying, 'I repent,' you shall forgive him."[30] She has been a living, breathing illustration of that.

Dr. John MacArthur said, "Forgiveness is the most Godlike act a person can do."[31] God has used my wife profoundly in my sanctification. Proverbs 18:22 says, "He who finds a wife finds a good thing, and obtains favor from the LORD."[32] She has definitely been a good thing to me! She truly is my best friend and the apple of my eye. She is my Proverbs 31 wife! "Strength and honor are her clothing; She shall rejoice in time to come. She opens her mouth with wisdom, and on her tongue is the law

28. Psalm 51:12 (New King James Version).

29. Second London Baptist Confession of Faith (1689), chap. 17, para. 3, in A Faith to Confess: The Baptist Confession of Faith of 1689 (Leeds: Carey Publications, 1975), 33

30. Luke 17:3-4 (New King James Version).

31. John MacArthur, The Freedom and Power of Forgiveness (Wheaton, IL: Crossway, 1998), 23.

32. Proverbs 18:22 (New King James Version).

of kindness. She watches over the ways of her household, and does not eat the bread of idleness. Her children rise up and call her blessed; Her husband also, and he praises her. 'Many daughters have done well, but you excel them all.' Charm is deceitful and beauty is passing. But a woman who fears the LORD, she shall be praised."[33]

We have been married for 10 years now (2025), and I can say that the last 5 have been the best! After moving from Virginia to Missouri, our marriage has gotten so much better. I remember seeing a brother from our old church at a G3 conference a couple of years after we moved. He was one of the men I used to meet with back in Virginia who helped counsel me in my marriage. He knew all the ugly details of my sin I had committed against my wife. At the conference, I was pushing around my two children, Tulip and London (Judah wasn't born yet), in a stroller. His jaw hit the floor when he saw me and the kids. He was astonished! Why? Because not only were Angie and I still married, but our marriage was flourishing, and we now had two beautiful children! He apparently wasn't expecting that. "Great are the works of the Lord; They are studied by all who delight in them."[34] His mercies are new every morning!

The Father's Immutable Love

I'm so thankful to God the Father for His gift of discipline! "Every good gift and every perfect gift is from above, and comes down from the Father of lights, with whom there is no variation or shadow of turning."[35] People say, "There's no love like a mother's love." Wrong, there's no love like the Father's! His love is perfect and unchanging. Zephaniah 3:17 says, "The Lord your God in your midst, the Mighty One, will save; He will rejoice over you with gladness, He will quiet you with His love, He will rejoice over you with singing."[36] Run to the Father through the Son now! He truly is the God of all comfort.[37]

---

33. Proverbs 31:25-30 (New King James Version).
34. Psalm 111:2 (New King James Version).
35. James 1:17 (New King James Version).
36. Zephaniah 3:17 (New King James Version).
37. 2 Corinthians 1:3 (New King James Version).

And Can It Be That I Should Gain

Words by Charles Wesley, 1738

And can it be that I should gain
An interest in the Savior's blood?
Died He for me, who caused His pain?
For me, who Him to death pursued?
Amazing love! How can it be
That Thou, my God, shouldst die for me?
Amazing love! How can it be
That Thou, my God, shouldst die for me?

He left His Father's throne above,
So free, so infinite His grace;
Emptied Himself of all but love,
And bled for Adam's helpless race;
'Tis mercy all, immense and free;
For, O my God, it found out me.
'Tis mercy all, immense and free;
For, O my God, it found out me.

Long my imprisoned spirit lay
Fast bound in sin and nature's night;
Thine eye diffused a quickening ray,
I woke, the dungeon flamed with light;
My chains fell off, my heart was free;
I rose, went forth, and followed Thee.
My chains fell off, my heart was free;
I rose, went forth, and followed Thee.

No condemnation now I dread;
Jesus, and all in Him, is mine!
Alive in Him, my living Head,
And clothed in righteousness divine,
Bold I approach the eternal throne,
And claim the crown, through Christ my own.
Bold I approach the eternal throne,
And claim the crown, through Christ my own.[38]

38. Charles Wesley, "And Can It Be That I Should Gain," in *Hymns and Sacred Poems* (London: Strahan, 1738), 105–7.

Chapter 8

To the Mosque with the Cross

"Do not answer a fool according to his folly, lest you also be like him. Answer a fool according to his folly, lest he be wise in his own eyes."[1]

The Qur'an vs the Qur'an

ONE FRIDAY AFTERNOON, MY dad and I drove to the Mosque, on the Old Dominion University (ODU) campus. This was the Mosque where my dad would normally go on Fridays for a special prayer. Friday (Jumu'ah in Arabic) is the holy day for Muslims. So, the reason we were driving to the Mosque was to have a meeting with the Imam. The Imam is basically the preacher for Muslims who leads the special prayer on Fridays. The Imam we met with this Friday was also a Professor at ODU.

Ever since my conversion I began witnessing to my dad and would ask him questions about Islam. Every time I would ask a question he couldn't answer he would say, "I don't know. Why don't we go ask the Imam?" I enjoyed that because it gave me many more opportunities to share the gospel with Muslims. I took full advantage of it. This particular time was to discuss a few passages in the Qur'an that I learned about.

Islam is a self-refuting religion. They believe that Allah sent down the Torah and the Gospel according to Surah 3:3-4.[2] James White, in his book

1. Proverbs 26:4–5 (New King James Version).
2. Qur'an 3:3-4, trans. Abdullah Yusuf Ali (New York: Tahrike Tarsile Qur'an, 2001).

What Every Christian Needs to Know About the Qur'an, says, "The Qur'an boldly claims that the revelation of God cannot be altered by man. Allah protects what he has sent down." See Surah 15:9, 6:114-115, 18:27 and 10:64 for example.[3] They also claim that the previous revelation that we Christians have, the Bible, was given by Allah but now has been corrupted. So, which is it? Does Allah preserve all his words or not? Some try to limit those texts to only be speaking about the Qur'an. I disagree with that interpretation and so do older Muslim Scholars. They would argue what has been distorted is the MEANING, not the text itself. But for the sake of argument let's say the text itself has been corrupted according to the Qur'an. In Surah 5:47 it says, "Let the People of the Gospel judge by that which Allah had revealed therein. Whoever judges not by that which Allah has revealed; such are the corrupt."[4] This text is saying Christians (People of the Gospel) are to Judge the Qur'an by previous revelation (The Bible). Guess what happens when you do that? You end up saying the Qur'an is FALSE.

Another problem Muslims run into is this. They claim the Bible has been corrupted. So, I asked the Imam, "When did that happen? Was it before those words were given in Surah 5 or after?" He didn't want to answer, just like my dad was unable to answer. Do you see the problem? If they claim the Bible was corrupted before those words were given, then you have Allah telling people to judge the Qur'an by a corrupt book. That's nonsensical. And if you claim the Bible was corrupted after those words were given then you have another problem. We have copies of the Bible that predate the Qur'an by centuries which demonstrate that the Bible we have today is the same Bible that existed during the time of Muhammad. The Bible has not been changed. Either way the Qur'an is refuted.

After talking with the Imam about those passages in the Qur'an I then went for the jugular. I simply said, "Mr. Imam, would you consider yourself to be a good person? Have you kept the Law of Moses the prophet?" I then took him through the Commandments. I told him that Isa (Jesus) the Prophet says if you have hate in your heart towards someone that is murder and if you look with lust at a woman you have committed adultery with her in your heart.[5] After I held up the Mirror of God's Law

---

3. James R. White, What Every Christian Needs to Know About the Qur'an (Minneapolis: Bethany House, 2013), 231; Qur'an 15:9, 6:114-115, 18:27, 10:64, trans. Abdullah Yusuf Ali

4. Qur'an 5:47, trans. Abdullah Yusuf Ali.

5. Matthew 5:21-22, 27-28 (New King James Version).

so he could see what he was in truth I then proceeded to tell him the Gospel. "For God so loved the world that He gave His only begotten Son, that whosoever believes in Him will not perish but will have everlasting life."[6] I explained how Jesus is truly God and truly Man. He kept God's Law on our behalf and took the punishment (wrath of God) that we deserve. He died on the cross and rose from the dead 3 days later. I let him know that if he would repent of his sin and place his trust in Christ alone, he would have everlasting life as a free gift. It can't be earned by us. It was earned by Christ and given to sinners by grace alone!

After hearing the gospel, he then wanted to talk about the Trinity and the Incarnation. The Trinity states that God is three in persons, Father, Son and Spirit, and one in being. He said, "How can God be three persons? That doesn't make sense." He then commented about God becoming a Man. "Are you telling me that God was hungry, got tired and went to the bathroom?" You see, to a Muslim those thoughts about God are offensive. I said the Bible teaches what we call the hypostatic union. Jesus had two natures, Divine and Human, in one person.

I then said to him, "Are you saying that because you cannot comprehend something about God then it isn't true?"

He nodded in agreement. I asked him, "Do you believe that God has always existed? God is eternal right? He has no beginning?"

He said, "Yes."

I said, "Can you comprehend that? Does that make sense to your finite mind?"

He then realized his dilemma. We had a wonderful exchange. There was no hatred or anger. He cared for me as I did for him. I gave him some literature, and he gave me a Qur'an. We left and it was quiet on the car ride home. I am pretty sure my dad realized that the reason he could not answer my questions I asked was because they cannot be answered. They show how the Qur'an contradicts itself. But logic and reason will not convert the sinner. They need the Holy Spirit for that.

The Blade That Never Dulles

Proverbs 26:5 says, "Answer a fool according to his folly, lest he be wise in his own eyes."[7] That is what I tried to do with the Imam. God's Word

6. John 3:16 (New King James Version).
7. Proverbs 26:5 (New King James Version).

truly is a lamp unto our feet and a light unto our path! Never lay it down, Christian! It is mighty indeed! God's Word is like a hammer that breaks the stony heart and a fire that purifies it. "For the word of God is living and powerful, and sharper than any two-edged sword, piercing even to the division of soul and spirit, and of joints and marrow, and is a discerner of the thoughts and intents of the heart. And there is no creature hidden from His sight, but all things are naked and open to the eyes of Him to whom we must give account."[8]

Not only did God save me from His wrath but he put a fire in my heart for the lost. If that is not another example of a good thing happening to a bad person, I don't know what is. Jesus told the disciples to follow Him and He would make them fishers of men.[9] That was not a suggestion, it was a promise from the God who cannot lie. So, if you ask me what my occupation is, I would say I'm a fisherman. And one thing I know about fishing is that fish don't jump into the boat. You have to throw the net into the water. So, I want to talk about one of the dirtiest words in the church today. You guessed it, the word is 'evangelism'.

Another word for 'evangelism' is the word 'love'. It is love in action. I believe one of the biggest reasons people do not share the gospel with lost people today is because they lack love. Their love has grown cold. They have left their first love. They have become noisy gongs and clanging symbols.[10] By God's grace I pray He ignites a fire in your heart for the lost that will never go out! I pray that you would say with the prophet Jeremiah, "Then I said, 'I will not make mention of Him, nor speak anymore in His name.' But His word was in my heart like a burning fire shut up in my bones; I was weary of holding it back, and I could not."[11] When things don't go well in witnessing encounters we can tend to get discouraged and do what Jeremiah wanted to do. Because of the persecution he experienced, he did not want to witness anymore. But God in His love did not let that happen.

.

8. Hebrews 4:12-13 (New King James Version).

9. Matthew 4:19 (New King James Version).

10. 1 Corinthians 13:1; Revelation 2:4 (New King James Version).

11. Jeremiah 20:9 (New King James Version).

When The Heart Grows Weary

Remember two things Christian, God's Word NEVER returns void, and your labor is not in vain in the Lord.[12] D.L. Moody, the famous evangelist, got discouraged. I will share a story about an encounter he once had concerning that, told by Harry Albus.

"One night when [Dwight L.] Moody was going home, it suddenly occurred to him that he had not spoken to a single person that day about accepting Christ. A day lost, he thought to himself. But as he walked up the street he saw a man by a lamppost. He promptly walked up to the man and asked, 'Are you a Christian?'. . .

"Nor did Moody find soul-winning easy. In fact, even Christians often criticized him for having 'zeal without knowledge.' Others called him 'Crazy Moody.' Once when he spoke to a perfect stranger about Christ, the man said, 'That is none of your business. . .If you were not a sort of a preacher I would knock you into the gutter for your impertinence.'

"The next day, a businessman friend sent for Moody. The businessman told Moody that the stranger he had spoken to was a friend of his. 'Moody, you've got zeal without knowledge: you insulted a friend of mine on the street last night. You went up to him, a perfect stranger, and asked him if he were a Christian.'

"Moody went out of his friend's office almost brokenhearted. For some time he worried about this. Then late one night a man pounded on the door of his home. It was the stranger he had supposedly insulted. The stranger said, 'Mr. Moody, I have not had a good night's sleep since that night you spoke to me under the lamppost, and I have come around at this unearthly hour of the night for you to tell me what I have to do to be saved.'"[13]

Do you want to witness but lack the expertise in apologetics? I mean, all you know is Jesus died for sinners, right? Are you weak (lacking trust in your own strength or ability)? Are you fearful (the thought scares you to death)? Do you tremble (aware of your insufficiency) just thinking about it? Well, you are in good company my friend! Listen to the Apostle Paul in 1 Corinthians 2:1-5. "And I, brethren, when I came to you, did not come with excellence of speech or of wisdom declaring to you the testimony of God. For I determined not to know anything among you

12. Isaiah 55:11; 1 Corinthians 15:58 (New King James Version).

13. Harry J. Albus, Twentieth Century Moody: The Biography of a Man and His Mission (Chicago: Moody Press, 1962), 87–88.

except Jesus Christ and Him crucified. I was with you in WEAKNESS, in FEAR, and in much TREMBLING. And my speech and my preaching were not with persuasive words of human wisdom, but in demonstration of the Spirit and of power, that your faith should not be in the wisdom of men but in the power of God."[14]

Do you remember when God told Moses to go and Moses said he basically wasn't a good talker? Remember how God responded? "So the LORD said to him, 'Who has made man's mouth? Or who makes the mute, the deaf, the seeing, or the blind? Have not I, the LORD? Now therefore, go, and I will be with your mouth and teach you what you shall say."[15] Never forget Christian, God is with us! And if He is with us and for us who can be against us? As someone once said 1 + God is a majority.

Shaming the Wise

God loves to use the foolish, weak and despised people of this world in order to shame the wise and mighty. 1 Corinthians 1:26-29 says this, "For you see your calling, brethren, that not many wise according to the flesh, not many mighty, not many noble, are called. But God has chosen the FOOL-ISH things of the world to put to shame the wise, and God has chosen the WEAK things of the world to put to shame the things which are mighty; and the base things of the world and the things which are DESPISED God has chosen, and the things which are not, to bring to nothing the things that are, that no flesh should glory in His presence."[16]

The men and women God has used throughout church history are those who knew they were nothing. In 2 Corinthians 12:11 Paul says, ". . .For in nothing was I behind the most eminent apostles, though I am nothing."[17] Martin Luther said, "God creates out of nothing. Therefore until man is nothing, God can make nothing out of him."[18] Do you see yourself that way? Are you nothing? Richard Wurmbrand, a Lutheran Pastor, who spent 14 years in prison for preaching the gospel, said this, "Clay is molded into a vessel, but the ultimate use of the vessel depends on the part where

14. 1 Corinthians 2:1-5 (New King James Version).

15. Exodus 4:11-12 (New King James Version).

16. 1 Corinthians 1:26-29 (New King James Version).

17. 2 Corinthians 12:11 (New King James Version).

18. Martin Luther, The Table Talk of Martin Luther, ed. Thomas S. Kepler (Grand Rapids: Baker Book House, 1979), 147.

nothing exists. Doors and windows are cut out of the wall of a house, but the ultimate use of the house depends on the parts where nothing exists. I wish to become such a useful nothing."[19]

So do what our Lord commanded us to do. . . Pray AND be the answer to prayer. Don't just lift up your hands to the Lord in worship; make sure you use them to reach out to the lost. "The harvest truly is plentiful, but the laborers are few. Therefore pray to the Lord of the harvest to send out laborers in His harvest."[20]

"Lift up your eyes and look at the fields Christian, for they are already white for harvest!"[21] We all will one day have things we regret, but there is one thing you will NEVER regret. . . Obeying Christ! He is WORTHY! Is it fair that we get to preach this glorious everlasting gospel? No, it is grace! I got to preach once shortly after my conversion when I was about 25 years old. I preached from Luke 16 about Lazarus and the Rich Man. After I was done preaching, I told everyone in the congregation to stand up. As they stood up, I said, "This sinful, weak, vile creature from the dust asked you to stand to your feet and you did. But when the Lord of glory tells you to go share the gospel. You say, 'No.' When the King of Kings says go into all the world and preach the gospel to every creature. You say, 'I think I will do something else.' Brothers and sisters, do me one favor. Stop listening to fallen men and spend the rest of your days listening to the Lord Jesus Christ who has ALL authority in heaven and on earth! He is WORTHY."[22]

19. Richard Wurmbrand, Tortured for Christ (Bartlesville, OK: Living Sacrifice Book Company, 1967), 34.

20. Matthew 9:37-38 (New King James Version).

21. John 4:35 (New King James Version).

22. Luke 16:19-31; Matthew 28:18-20 (New King James Version).

Hark, the Voice of Jesus Calling

Words by Daniel March, 1868

Hark, the voice of Jesus calling,
"Who will go and work today?
Fields are white, and harvests waiting,
Who will bear the sheaves away?"
Loud and long the Master calleth,
Rich reward He offers free;
Who will answer, gladly saying,
"Here am I, send me, send me"?

If you cannot cross the ocean,
And the heathen lands explore,
You can find the heathen nearer,
You can help them at your door;
If you cannot give your thousands,
You can give the widow's mite;
And the least you give for Jesus
Will be precious in His sight.

If you cannot speak like angels,
If you cannot preach like Paul,
You can tell the love of Jesus,
You can say He died for all;
If you cannot rouse the wicked
With the judgment's dread alarms,
You can lead the little children
To the Savior's waiting arms.

Let none hear you idly saying,
"There is nothing I can do,"
While the souls of men are dying,
And the Master calls for you;
Take the task He gives you gladly,
Let His work your pleasure be;
Answer quickly when He calleth,
"Here am I, send me, send me!"[23]

23. Daniel March, "Hark, the Voice of Jesus Calling," in *Hymns for the Anniversary of the Boston Young Men's Christian Association* (Boston: T.R. Marvin & Son, 1868), 12–13.

Chapter 9

Paradox

"If I had the power of God, there are many things that I would change; but if I had the wisdom of God, I would not change a thing." Unknown[1]

Behold God's Wisdom

THE CHRISTIAN LIFE IS a paradox in many ways. In the *Valley of Vision*, a collection of Puritan prayers and devotions, it says this in the introduction: "LORD, HIGH AND HOLY, MEEK AND LOWLY, Thou hast brought me to the valley of vision, where I live in the depths but see thee in the heights; hemmed in by mountains of sin I behold thy glory.

> Let me learn by paradox
> that the way down is the way up,
> that to be low is to be high,
> that the broken heart is the healed heart,
> that the contrite spirit is the rejoicing spirit,
> that the repenting soul is the victorious soul,
> that to have nothing is to possess all,
> that to bear the cross is to wear the crown,

---

1. Author unknown, quoted in The Valley of Vision: A Collection of Puritan Prayers and Devotions, ed. Arthur Bennett (Carlisle, PA: Banner of Truth Trust, 1975), xxi.

that to give is to receive,

that the valley is the place of vision.

Lord, in the daytime stars can be seen from deepest wells,

and the deeper the wells the brighter thy stars shine;

Let me find thy light in my darkness,

thy life in my death,

thy joy in my sorrow,

thy grace in my sin,

thy riches in my poverty,

thy glory in my valley."[2]

I used to wish my life would have gone differently. I would say things to myself like, "I wish I had gone to Dive School when I was in the Navy instead of being a dumb teenager who lost that opportunity because he liked throwing eggs at cars."

Or, "I wish I was still a Norfolk Firefighter. What an honorable job that was to have which gained me much respect. I definitely wish I had never got arrested, went to jail and had to suffer the consequences of that by being a convicted felon and registered sex offender." Looking back now I can truly say I am thankful to God for His Gracious Sovereign hand in it all! He used those events in my life providentially to make me the man I am today. As Paul said, "But by the grace of God, I am what I am."[3] They shaped me and molded me in ways I could never have imagined. Plus, I would have never met my beautiful bride Angie and had three wonderful children with her. Maybe that's why I love the movie It's a Wonderful Life so much. I truly am the "richest man in the world."[4] "For all things are yours: whether Paul or Apollos or Cephas, or the world or life or death, or things present or things to come—all are yours." 1 Corinthians 3:21-22

A Bold Fool

I can relate to many characters in the Bible but the one I identify with the most is Peter. He was impulsive, passionate and bold. He would often

2. The Valley of Vision, ed. Arthur Bennett, xx–xxi.

3. 1 Corinthians 15:10 (New King James Version).

4. It's a Wonderful Life, directed by Frank Capra (Hollywood, CA: Liberty Films, 1946), film.

act or speak without thinking. I have also been compared to the great reformer Martin Luther. It wasn't a compliment. He was known as a bull in a china shop. One thing I find comforting is that we are one way when we come to know the Lord and over time we become more like Christ. It is a lifelong process that will one day end in glorification. He is the Potter after all, and we are but clay.[5]

I find the Apostle Peter so encouraging in this regard. He had such a great love for our Lord and was at the same time a man of great weaknesses and folly. He wanted to go where the Lord went and do what He did! Peter was a fisherman when the Lord called him. It is recorded in Matthew 4:18-20: "And Jesus, walking by the Sea of Galilee, saw two brothers, Simon called Peter, and Andrew his brother, casting a net into the sea; for they were fishermen. Then He said to them, 'Follow Me, and I will make you fishers of men.' They immediately left their nets and followed Him."[6]

Peter also had a desire to follow the Lord into the realm of the supernatural. We read about it in Matthew 14:25-31: "Now in the fourth watch of the night Jesus went to them, walking on the sea. And when the disciples saw Him walking on the sea, they were troubled, saying, 'It is a ghost!' And they cried out for fear. But immediately Jesus spoke to them, saying, 'Be of good cheer! It is I; do not be afraid.' And Peter answered Him and said, 'Lord, if it is You, command me to come to You on the water.' So, He said, 'Come.' And when Peter had come down out of the boat, he walked on the water to go to Jesus. But when he saw that the wind was boisterous, he was afraid; and beginning to sink he cried out, saying, 'Lord, save me!' And immediately Jesus stretched out His hand and caught him, and said to him, 'O you of little faith, why did you doubt?'"[7]

Later on, in the gospel of Matthew, Jesus asked his disciples "Who do men say that I am." After they answered Him, He asked them "Who do you say that I am?" Peter gave the right answer because the Father in heaven revealed it to him. Even after Peter answered rightly and was blessed by the Lord he ended up getting rebuked just 7 verses later by Christ. "But He (Christ) turned and said to Peter, 'Get behind Me, Satan! You are an offense to Me, for you are not mindful of the things of God,

5. Isaiah 64:8 (New King James Version).

6. Matthew 4:18-20 (New King James Version).

7. Matthew 14:25-31 (New King James Version).

but the things of men.'"[8] Peter was a hot mess before AND after he came to know Christ. God is truly longsuffering!

Peter also experienced the most glorious thing ever! The transfiguration of Christ! He was on the Mount of Transfiguration when Christ "was transfigured before them as His face shone like the sun, and His clothes became as white as the light." Moses and Elijah also appeared as they talked with Christ. Peter opened his big mouth and wanted to make 3 tabernacles for each of them. While Peter was still speaking God the Father interrupted him and rebuked him. "While he was still speaking, behold, a bright cloud overshadowed them; and suddenly a voice came out of the cloud, saying, 'THIS is My beloved Son, in whom I am well pleased. Hear HIM!' And when the disciples heard it, they fell on their faces and were greatly afraid."[9] God was saying to Peter, don't put Moses and Elijah in the same category as Christ. They are *simul justus et peccator*, simultaneously sinful and justified. Not so with My Son! He is the sinless, spotless Lamb of God!

But God

Then we see Peter again say with boldness that he will NEVER deny His Lord, even if everyone else does. "Then Jesus said to them, 'All of you will be made to stumble because of Me this night, for it is written: "I will strike the Shepherd, And the sheep of the flock will be scattered." But after I have been raised, I will go before you to Galilee.' Peter answered and said to Him, 'Even if all are made to stumble because of You, I will never be made to stumble.' Jesus said to him, 'Assuredly, I say to you that this night, before the rooster crows, you will deny Me three times.' Peter said to Him, 'Even if I have to die with You, I will not deny You!' And so said all the disciples."[10] He had such a love for his Lord, but he also had confidence in his flesh. He didn't realize how weak his flesh was.

One of the most beautiful scenes is in the last chapter of John. Can you imagine how you would feel if you were Peter? He denied His Lord 3 times. He realized how weak he truly was. So, at this point he does what you would expect him to do. He quits the ministry. He says, I am going back to what I know, fishing. "Simon Peter said to them, 'I am going fishing.' They also said to him, 'We are going with you also.' They went out and

8. Matthew 16:13-16, 22-23 (New King James Version).
9. Matthew 17:2-6 (New King James Version).
10. Matthew 26:31-35 (New King James Version).

got into the boat, and that night they caught NOTHING."[11] He couldn't even do his old job well anymore. Then we see our great God who is full of compassion and mercy approach one of His beloved lambs. This is what He says to him. "So when they had eaten breakfast, Jesus said to Simon Peter, 'Simon, son of Jonah, do you love Me more than these?' He said to Him, 'Yes, Lord; You know that I love You.' He said to him, 'Feed My lambs.' He said to him again a second time, 'Simon, son of Jonah, do you love Me?' He said to Him, 'Yes, Lord; You know that I love You.' He said to him, 'Tend My sheep.' He said to him the third time, 'Simon, son of Jonah, do you love Me?' Peter was grieved because He said to him the third time, 'Do you love Me?' And he said to Him, 'Lord, You know all things; You know that I love You.' Jesus said to him, 'Feed My sheep. Most assuredly, I say to you, when you were younger, you girded yourself and walked where you wished; but when you are old, you will stretch out your hands, and another will gird you and carry you where you do not wish.' This He spoke, signifying by what death he would glorify God. And when He had spoken this, He said to him, 'Follow Me.'"[12]

Being a disciple of Christ is not about how strong we are. It is actually about how weak we are. Our weakness is our strength. The Apostle Paul says this in 2 Cor. 12:7-10: "And lest I should be exalted above measure by the abundance of the revelations, a thorn in the flesh was given to me, a messenger of Satan to buffet me, lest I be exalted above measure. Concerning this thing I pleaded with the Lord three times that it might depart from me. And He said to me, 'My grace is sufficient for you, for My strength is made perfect in weakness.' Therefore most gladly I will rather boast in my infirmities, that the power of Christ may rest upon me. Therefore I take pleasure in infirmities, in reproaches, in needs, in persecutions, in distresses, for Christ's sake. For when I am weak, then I am strong."[13]

Still Learning

Even after this beautiful scene of Peter being restored by the Lord you would have thought, surely, he learned his lesson by now. Nope, he still had indwelling sin which manifested in the fear of man. The Apostle Paul had to rebuke Peter publicly in Antioch because he was not being

11. John 21:3 (New King James Version).
12. John 21:15-19 (New King James Version).
13. 2 Corinthians 12:7-10 (New King James Version).

straightforward about the truth of the gospel. Here is the account recorded in Galatians 2:11-16: "Now when Peter had come to Antioch, I withstood him to his face, because he was to be blamed; for before certain men came from James, he would eat with the Gentiles; but when they came, he withdrew and separated himself, fearing those who were of the circumcision. And the rest of the Jews also played the hypocrite with him, so that even Barnabas was carried away with their hypocrisy.

"But when I saw that they were not straightforward about the truth of the gospel, I said to Peter before them all, 'If you, being a Jew, live in the manner of Gentiles and not as the Jew, why do you compel Gentiles to live as Jews? We who are Jews by nature, and not sinners of the Gentiles, knowing that a man is not justified by the works of the law but by faith in Jesus Christ, even we have believed in Christ Jesus, that we might be justified by faith in Christ and not by the works of the law; for by the works of the law no flesh shall be justified.'"[14]

Peter is a wonderful example of how God's grace is sufficient, and His strength is made perfect in weakness. Your greatest strength is your weakness. The problem is most of us believe we are strong. Think about this for a second. If I asked you, how is your prayer life? You might say, "Not that good. I need to pray more but I am just so weak." I would actually say your problem is not that you are so weak, but you believe you are so strong.

The person who knows he is weak is the one who says, "I have to pray! I must pray! I will die without it!" A prayerless Christian is an oxymoron. Martin Luther once said, "To be a Christian without prayer is no more possible than to be alive without breathing."[15] Most people tend to shorten their prayer time or Bible reading when they have a busy day. But that should not be so! Luther also said, "I have so much to do [today] that I should spend the first three hours in prayer."[16]

14. Galatians 2:11-16 (New King James Version).

15. Ray Comfort, ed., *The Evidence Study Bible: New King James Version* (Alachua, FL: Bridge-Logos Publishers, 2011), 1222, quoting Martin Luther.

16. Ray Comfort, ed., *The Evidence Study Bible: New King James Version* (Alachua, FL: Bridge-Logos Publishers, 2011), 1389, quoting Martin Luther.

God's Sovereign Hand

I wonder if Peter ever thought "I wished my life went differently than it did." Whether he did or didn't doesn't matter. In order for Peter to be filled by the Spirit he had to be emptied of self.

D.L. Moody said, "God sends no one away empty, except those who are full of themselves."[17] Was it fair that Peter was forgiven over and over again? Nope, that is grace! I remember once listening to a sermon by Leonard Ravenhill where he talked about Moses.

He said, as only Leonard Ravenhill could say, "God took Moses out of Egypt and then spent the next 40 years taking Egypt out of Moses."[18] God is sovereign! Proverbs 21:1 says, "The king's heart is in the hand of the LORD, like rivers of water; He turns it wherever He wishes."[19] God even uses our sin sinlessly, as Joseph said to his brothers, "You meant evil against me, God meant it for good."[20]

Our greatest need is to know who God is. Here is how the London confession of 1689 answers that: "The Lord our God is one, the only living and true God. He is self-existent and infinite in being and perfection. His essence cannot be understood by anyone but Him. He is a perfectly pure spirit. He is invisible and has no body, parts, or changeable emotions. He alone has immortality, dwelling in light that no one can approach. He is unchangeable, immense, eternal, incomprehensible, almighty, in every way infinite, absolutely holy, perfectly wise, wholly free, completely absolute. He works all things according to the counsel of His own unchangeable and completely righteous will for His own glory. He is most loving, gracious, merciful, and patient. He overflows with goodness and truth, forgiving iniquity, transgression, and sin. He rewards those who seek Him diligently. At the same time, He is perfectly just and terrifying in His judgements. He hates all sin and will certainly not clear the guilty."[21] That is who God is! He is Yahweh the triune God! There is NONE like Him!

---

17. Dwight L. Moody, quoted in Moody's Anecdotes and Illustrations (Chicago: Rhodes & McClure Publishing, 1898), 127.

18. Leonard Ravenhill, "The Cost of Discipleship," sermon, n.d., https://www.sermonaudio.com/sermoninfo.asp?SID=101506154150.

19. Proverbs 21:1 (New King James Version).

20. Genesis 50:20 (New King James Version).

21. Second London Baptist Confession of Faith (1689), chap. 2, in A Faith to Confess: The Baptist Confession of Faith of 1689 (Leeds: Carey Publications, 1975), 5–6.

So, remember the words of Peter, "Be sober, vigilant; because your adversary the devil walks about like a roaring lion, seeking whom he may devour. Resist him, steadfast in the faith, knowing that the same sufferings are experienced by your brotherhood in the world. But may the God of all grace, who called us to His eternal glory by Christ Jesus, after you have suffered a while, perfect, establish, strengthen, and settle you. To Him be the glory and the dominion forever and ever. Amen."[22]

22. 1 Peter 5:8-11 (New King James Version).

It Is Well with My Soul
Words by Horatio G. Spafford, 1873

When peace, like a river, attendeth my way,
When sorrows like sea billows roll;
Whatever my lot, Thou hast taught me to say,
It is well, it is well with my soul.

Though Satan should buffet, though trials should come,
Let this blest assurance control,
That Christ hath regarded my helpless estate,
And hath shed His own blood for my soul.

My sin—oh, the bliss of this glorious thought!—
My sin, not in part but the whole,
Is nailed to the cross, and I bear it no more,
Praise the Lord, praise the Lord, O my soul![23]

23. Horatio G. Spafford, "It Is Well with My Soul," in *Sacred Songs No. 1*, ed. Ira D. Sankey, Philip P. Bliss, and others (New York: Biglow & Main, 1876), no. 42.

Chapter 10

The Ugliest Sin in the Bible

"Brother, if any man thinks ill of you, do not be angry with him; for you are worse than he thinks you to be. If he charges you falsely on some point, yet be satisfied, for if he knew you better he might change the accusation, and you would be no gainer by the correction. If you have your moral portrait painted, and it is ugly, be satisfied; for it only needs a few blacker touches, and it would be still nearer the truth." Spurgeon[1]

A Sniper Misses the Mark

IT WAS A BEAUTIFUL sunny day in Virginia Beach. I was out driving my truck for work with my 24-foot ladder on top heading to my next appointment. I pulled up to the next address, hopped out of my truck and walked up to the front door. I rang the doorbell and this military looking man came to the door. I let him know who I was and why I was there. He gave me the thumbs up, and I got to work.

After I measured everything, I wrote up an estimate for a new roof. I walked back up to his front door and he came outside to discuss the estimate. As we are talking, I found out he was in the military in special forces. He was a man's man. He was good looking, sharp, chiseled, and

1. Charles H. Spurgeon, "The Lesson of the Forge," in Metropolitan Tabernacle Pulpit (London: Passmore & Alabaster, 1882), 28:452.

well spoken. Come to find out he was a sniper. As he described his job, he expressed his anger towards our enemies overseas and let me know he has been very successful in doing his job. He used more colorful language than I would care to repeat. I asked if he ever came close to dying in the field. He said, "Yes, more than once."

I then asked what he thought would have happened to him if he did die. Where would he go? He said, "In the ground."

I said, "So you will become worm food and that is it?"

He said, "Yep." So, I asked if he was an atheist. He nodded his head and said he was. I knew I was in for a battle at this point. He was a very proud and arrogant man in his demeanor.

I have spoken with Navy Seals before who were extremely self-righteous, and this gentleman had the same aroma. Virginia Beach is home to Seal Team 2, 4, 8 and 10. You run into them more often than you would expect. After asking more questions about why he was an atheist, what is his ultimate authority, does he really believe in the scientific impossibility that NOTHING created everything, I said to myself, "Enough playing games, time to get out the big guns!"

So, I addressed his conscience. I said, "Would you consider yourself to be a good person? IF there is a heaven, do you think you would go there when you die?"

His response was expected. He said, "Of course I am a good person, and I believe I would make it." So, I took him through the Ten Commandments to shut his mouth (Romans 3:19).[2] I fired those 10 cannons at him one by one. He was not happy about it, but I knew it was necessary. James 4:6 says, "God resists the proud but gives grace to the humble."[3] This man needed to be humbled by the Law. So, I continued out of love for him and zeal for God's glory.

After helping him see how he had broken God's Law and was guilty, I asked if he would still go to heaven.

He said, "Yes I would" and then proceeded to tell me how much of a hero he was for taking out the "bad" guys, whom he despised. He was the good guy you see. He had earned his forgiveness by killing the enemy. I then shared the court analogy with him.

I said, "Try that in a court of law my friend. In court you are judged for what you do wrong, not for what you supposedly do right. Your 'good'

2. Romans 3:19 (New King James Version).
3. James 4:6 (New King James Version).

deeds are nothing more than 'splendid sins' as Augustine once said.[4] I told him that is like pleading with the Judge, 'Your honor, I just want you to know that I washed your car this morning and cut your grass. I also slipped a 100-dollar bill in your coat pocket. Now won't you please let me go.' If he is a good Judge he will throw the book at you. Not only for breaking the law but also for trying to bribe him in the process."

At this point he became very angry and told me it was time for me to go. He said, "If God will punish me as an American soldier who loves my country by defending her then I want nothing to do with Him."

I said, "I know you don't. That is why I am talking with you. The gospel is offensive. It says we are ALL bad guys. There is none righteous, not even snipers."[5] I thanked him for his time and got back in my truck. I prayed for him and headed off to my next appointment.

Despising Others

His story is not uncommon. It reminds me of one of my favorite parables Jesus told in the gospel of Luke. Luke 18:9-14 says, "Also He (Jesus) spoke this parable to some who trusted in themselves that they were righteous, and despised others: 'Two men went up to the temple to pray, one a Pharisee and the other a tax collector. The Pharisee stood and prayed thus with himself, "God, I thank You that I am not like other men—extortioners, unjust, adulterers, or even as this tax collector. I fast twice a week; I give tithes of all that I possess." And the tax collector, standing afar off, would not so much as raise his eyes to heaven, but beat his breast, saying, "God, be merciful to me, a sinner!" I tell you, this man went down to his house justified rather than the other; for everyone who exalts himself will be humbled, and he who humbles himself will be exalted.'"[6]

I share this parable to highlight something very important. The heart that says, "that's not fair" tends to despise others, while thinking "I'm a good person." THAT is the heart of the matter. The parable of the Pharisee and the tax collector display this marvelously. The Pharisee thanks God that he is not like other men. He says to God, in essence, those are the bad guys, and I am the good guy. Self-righteousness is the ugliest sin in the entire Bible. Charles

---

4. Ray Comfort, ed., *The Evidence Study Bible: New King James Version* (Alachua, FL: Bridge-Logos Publishers, 2011), 862, quoting Augustine.

5. Romans 3:10 (New King James Version).

6. Luke 18:9-14 (New King James Version).

Spurgeon once said, "Nothing can damn a man but his own righteousness; nothing can save him but the righteousness of Christ."[7] The sniper's attitude is the attitude we are ALL born with. What is our attitude when we hear about a pedophile who has done wicked things or a rapist? What about a murderer or a homosexual? Is our attitude like the Pharisee who despises those people and thanks God that he is not like them? Or do we respond like the tax collector, who knows he has a wicked heart, and beats his breast as he cries out to God, "Be merciful to me THE sinner!"

Think of King David. He was the king of Israel who had power, women and riches. He killed a lion, a giant and a bear; Oh my! (I am a dad, what can I say.) He was a man of war with an impressive record. I mean, the women did sing "Saul has slain his thousands, and David his tens of thousands" right?[8] Pride has a way of making us think we are something when we are nothing. So, one day instead of going to battle like he normally would, David remained in Jerusalem. One evening he saw a woman named Bathsheba, who was very beautiful, taking a bath. David sent his messengers to get her for him so he could sleep with her. After he slept with her, he sent her back home and found out later that she was pregnant with his child. David made a plan to cover up his sin. Bathsheba's husband, Uriah was away from home for the battle, so David brought him back for a time, hoping he would sleep with his wife and think that the child is his. But Uriah was an honorable soldier who refused to sleep with his wife during the time of war. So, when he went back to the battle, David gave orders to have him put in the front and have the other soldiers retreat. David's plan worked. Uriah was killed.

9 months to a year later, Nathan the prophet was sent by the Lord to confront David about his sin. Here is the confrontation from 2 Samuel 12:1-7: "Then the Lord sent Nathan to David. And he came to him, and said to him: 'There were two men in one city, one rich and the other poor. The rich man had exceedingly many flocks and herds. But the poor man had nothing, except one little ewe lamb which he had bought and nourished; and it grew up together with him and with his children. It ate of his own food and drank from his own cup and lay in his bosom; and it was like a daughter to him. And a traveler came to the rich man, who refused to take from his own flock and from his own herd to prepare one for the

---

7. Ray Comfort, ed., *The Evidence Study Bible: New King James Version* (Alachua, FL: Bridge-Logos Publishers, 2011), 881, quoting Charles Spurgeon.

8. 1 Samuel 18:7 (New King James Version).

wayfaring man who had come to him; but he took the poor man's lamb and prepared it for the man who had come to him.' So David's anger was greatly aroused against the man, and he said to Nathan, 'As the Lord lives, the man who has done this shall surely die! And he shall restore fourfold for the lamb, because he did this thing and because he had no pity.' Then Nathan said to David, 'YOU are the man!'"[9]

Compassion Needed

How many of us become like David? We commit great sin and may even hide it for a time. After some time passes by, we encounter some gross sin "out there" and we become angry like David did towards the supposed offender, who was really him. An unrepentant heart is fertile ground for self-righteousness to grow. When we remember that OUR sins are gross, we will have love and compassion for the offender, not hatred. We will then be able to speak the truth to them in love. We will no longer despise them but pray for them. We won't wish for fire to come down from heaven and destroy them, but we will plead with them to come to Christ. We will begin to be more like the Apostle Paul who said, "I have great sorrow and continual grief in my heart. For I could wish that I myself were accursed from Christ for my brethren, my countrymen according to the flesh."[10]

As I spoke with the professing atheist, you may have wondered why I didn't present evidence to "prove" God's existence or on the other hand, why didn't I show him how He can't know anything without the God. Well, I chose not to spend time doing either of those because neither of those methods will bring about his conversion. That is why I addressed his conscience. There is an ally in every human's heart, and it is his God given conscience. "They show that the work of the law is written on their hearts, while their conscience also bears witness, and their conflicting thoughts accuse or even excuse them."[11] What a blessing from the Lord! Plus, what if I did prove to his satisfaction that God exists or what if I showed him how he really can't know anything without God? I might have changed his mind about those things, but not his heart. He needed to hear the gospel. The gospel is the power of God unto salvation![12]

9. 2 Samuel 12:1-7 (New King James Version).

10. Romans 9:2-3 (New King James Version).

11. Romans 2:15 (New King James Version).

12. Romans 1:16 (New King James Version).

Without Excuse

Two stories illustrate this point. My stepdaughter Jordan who is a professing transgender (I say professing because there is no such thing as a transgender) used to go to church with us back when she was a teenager. She and I have had several conversations about the Bible, God and the gospel up to this point. She did not reject the gospel because she needed more evidence. It was not an intellectual problem she was having. It was a sin problem. She loved her sin and hated God. So, at church one Sunday morning after the service was over one of the ladies who befriended her was talking with her about the Bible. I walked up and she was telling Jordan about all the manuscript evidence we have for the Bible and how you can trust it etc. All good and true. I interrupted briefly and said, "May I ask Jordan one question and then you can continue on with y'all's conversation?"

She said, "Of course."

I said, "Jordan, if Christianity were true would you become a Christian?"

Jordan did not hesitate for a moment and said, "No."

I said, "There you have it. You can continue talking."

I am not against apologetics at all. In fact, I use them all the time. I also know that every person I meet has the same problem: Sin against a holy God and the only solution is Christ and Him crucified. So, I want to get to the Law and Gospel as fast as I can. That is my objective in every encounter I have. Spurgeon once said, "Preach Christ or nothing: don't dispute or discuss except with your eye on the cross."[13] The Apostle Paul said a similar thing, "For I determined to know nothing among you except Jesus Christ and Him crucified!"[14]

Another story that comes to mind is about my stepson, Dylan, from a few years ago. Dylan is the nicest guy you will ever meet. He just likes to argue about everything. I mean EVERYTHING. . . He and I have had so many conversations about Christianity, it is not funny. Every time we spoke, I would say to myself, I just answered his objection, now he has to believe, right? Wrong. His problem was not intellectual either. He knows God exists just like every person on the planet does, he just doesn't love

---

13. Ray Comfort, ed., *The Evidence Study Bible: New King James Version* (Alachua, FL: Bridge-Logos Publishers, 2011), 1703, quoting Charles Spurgeon.

14. 1 Corinthians 2:2 (New King James Version).

God. He suppresses the truth in unrighteousness because he loves his sin.[15] That is EVERY unbeliever's problem.

So, after talking to Dylan over and over about God, I heard a great parable that really summed up his dilemma. No amount of evidence would change his mind. I told him that. So, I shared this parable with him. I said, "There once was a man who believed he was dead. He was really convinced of it. No matter how much he talked to other people about it they couldn't convince him otherwise. So, he finally went to the doctor to see if he could help him. The doctor did test after test on him showing how dead people don't have brain waves, or they don't walk and talk etc. But the man kept giving reasons about how it has been shown in studies that even after people die there is still brain activity that goes on and so forth. So, the doctor asked him, 'Do dead people bleed?' The man thought about it for a moment. Then he looked at the doctor and said, 'No they don't.' So, the doctor grabbed the man's hand really quick and pricked his finger. Blood started gushing out. The man grabbed his finger and looked up at the doctor and said, 'Wow! I guess dead people DO bleed!'" Dylan always gets a chuckle out of that story, but that is the fact of the matter. Unbelievers are "dead in their trespasses and sins."[16] No amount of reasoning will bring them to life. They must be born again![17]

Run to Them

I pray that as you read this book about really bad sinners like me, you will see how great of a Savior we have in Christ! Is it fair? No, it is grace! Instead of being like Jonah who despised the Ninevites, may you become more like Christ who died for them![18] Instead of trusting in yourself while despising others, imitate God who NEVER despises a broken and contrite heart![19] Let us, by God's grace, cast off the self-righteous attitude of the older brother and let us put on the mercy and grace of the father from the story of the two lost sons![20] Stop despising sinners and start running to them! All of heaven

15. Romans 1:18 (New King James Version).
16. Ephesians 2:1 (New King James Version).
17. John 3:3 (New King James Version).
18. Jonah 4:1-3; Matthew 20:28 (New King James Version).
19. Psalm 51:17 (New King James Version).
20. Luke 15:11-32 (New King James Version).

rejoices when one sinner repents![21] Let us do likewise! "Now to the King eternal, immortal, invisible, to God who alone is wise, be honor and glory forever and ever. Amen."[22]

21. Luke 15:7 (New King James Version).

22. 1 Timothy 1:17 (New King James Version).

How Sweet and Awful is the Place
Written by Isaac Watts, 1776

How sweet and awful is the place
With Christ within the doors,
While everlasting love displays
The choicest of her stores!

Here ev'ry Bowel of our God
With soft Compassion rolls;
Here Peace and Pardon bought with Blood,
Is Food for dying Souls.

While all our hearts and all our songs
Join to admire the feast,
Each of us cry, with thankful tongues,
"Lord, why was I a guest?"

"Why was I made to hear Thy voice,
And enter while there's room,
When thousands make a wretched choice,
And rather starve than come?"

'Twas the same love that spread the feast
That sweetly drew us in;
Else we had still refused to taste,
And perished in our sin.

Pity the nations, O our God!
Constrain the earth to come;
Send Thy victorious Word abroad,
And bring the strangers home.

We long to see Thy churches full,
That all the chosen race
May with one voice, and heart, and soul,
Sing Thy redeeming grace.[23]

23. Isaac Watts, "How Sweet and Awful Is the Place," in Hymns and Spiritual Songs (London: J. Buckland, 1776), no. 94.

Chapter 11

Good to All

"See what wickedness there is in the nature of man. How much are we beholden to the restraining grace of God! For, were it not for this, man, who was made but a little lower than angels, would make himself a great deal lower than the devils." Matthew Henry[1]

The Gift of Common Grace

THERE ALWAYS SEEMS TO be certain doctrines that are debated amongst Christians. One of those is the doctrine known as Common Grace. I thought this was pretty obvious, but what do I know? I mean, who can deny God's general kindness towards all people everywhere? But I think I can settle the debate once and for all. Before we go to Scripture I would like to give just one example. The irrefutable, undeniable, evidence for Common Grace is. . . TACO BELL! Yep, that settles the matter once and for all. In fact, I should just end the chapter now.

This doctrine demonstrates the goodness of God towards all His creation. I believe we see that clearly taught in the Noahic Covenant. In Genesis 6 God destroyed the world with a flood except for eight people. Once the floodwaters subsided, Noah and his family disembarked from the ark. The LORD God then made a covenant with Noah, his family and EVERY

1. Ray Comfort, ed., *The Evidence Study Bible: New King James Version* (Alachua, FL: Bridge-Logos Publishers, 2011), 708, quoting Matthew Henry.

living creature. This was an unconditional covenant. This was a covenant of preservation or as some like to call it, a covenant of common grace. God made this covenant with ALL mankind, believer and unbeliever. This is the foundation for common grace.[2]

Every single person born experiences this kind of grace. We all share the same sun, moon and stars. We all receive the same rain and snow. Charles Spurgeon said, "He maketh His sun to rise on the evil and on the good, and sendeth rain on the just and on the unjust—oh, the greatness of His heart that He should thus deal even with those who despise Him!"[3] God has provided EVERYTHING for EVERYONE. This is who He is. He is a merciful God, whose mercies are new EVERY morning![4]

The Gift of Restraining Grace

Another aspect of common grace is when God restrains evil. Every human being is evil by nature but because of God's restraining grace we do not act as evil as we could. We see God doing this in Genesis 20:6 with Abimelech, king of Gerar. "Then God said to him in the dream, 'Yes, I know that you did this in the integrity of your heart. For I also withheld you from sinning against Me; therefore I did not let you touch her.'"[5] Spurgeon once said, "Were it not for the restraining hand of God, the world would long ago have been a den of wild beasts; His mercy keeps back the full flood of human wickedness."[6]

At one of my roofing appointments, I met a middle-aged Filipino man. He was very kind when I first met him. After we discussed the roof estimate we began talking about God and the Bible. He was a very passionate man and spoke highly of the Bible. I thought, "Maybe this guy is really a Christian." As we talked further, I realized he wasn't a Christian. He believed he was saved by works and denied the deity of Jesus Christ. He belonged to a Cult that originated in the Philippines called Iglesia ni

2. Genesis 9:8-17 (New King James Version).

3. Charles H. Spurgeon, "God's Thoughts and Ways Far Above Ours," in Metropolitan Tabernacle Pulpit (London: Passmore & Alabaster, 1887), 33:412.

4. Lamentations 3:22-23 (New King James Version).

5. Genesis 20:6 (New King James Version).

6. Charles H. Spurgeon, "The Restraining Prayer," in Metropolitan Tabernacle Pulpit (London: Passmore & Alabaster, 1879), 25:398.

Cristo. They would describe themselves as a restoration of the original church established by Jesus Christ.

After we talked for a while, he invited me to speak further with his elders about this. He wanted me to come to one of their services. I told him I wouldn't go to his church, but we could meet up again with Bibles in hand and talk. He got my phone number and said he would get back to me. Later he called and said two of the men from his church would be willing to meet in his home with me. I told him I would like to bring my pastor along with me. He agreed to that.

So, one Tuesday afternoon, Pastor and I grabbed dinner at Texas Roadhouse and then headed to my customer's house for the debate. I asked if we could limit the discussion to just one specific topic for the sake of time. They agreed and we discussed the deity of Christ. They were very similar to how the Jehovah Witnesses argued with one major difference. They did not have their own new fabricated translation. We had the same Bible. It was great! We discussed passage after passage which clearly without doubt proclaimed the deity of Christ. The gentleman who invited me over was getting more frustrated as the night went on.

After talking for a while with them it dawned on me how simplistic they were in their reading of the Bible. Similar to how Muslims will say, "Where does Jesus say, 'I am God, worship Me' in the Bible?" Well, those exact words are not there, but that truth is clearly there. The Bible is incredibly profound when it comes to the deity of Christ! In the Old Testament the covenant name for God is Yahweh. There are passages in the Old Testament which speak about Yahweh such as in Isaiah 6 or Psalm 102. The New Testament authors will then quote those passages and say they are talking about Jesus, which clearly means Jesus is Yahweh! It is wonderful![7]

At one point in the conversation, I asked them to turn to Isaiah 9:6. This is the famous Christmas card verse that everyone knows is about Jesus. We looked at it together. I began reading it "For unto us a Child is born, unto us a Son is given; and the government will be upon His shoulder, and His name will be called Wonderful, Counselor, Mighty God. . ." I stopped and said, "You see right there in this passage the Prophet Isaiah calls Jesus the Mighty God."[8] When I said that the man who invited me over stood up and began yelling at me about how Jesus is not God. His elder and one of

7. Isaiah 6:1-5; Psalm 102:25-27; John 12:41; Hebrews 1:10-12 (New King James Version).

8. Isaiah 9:6 (New King James Version).

his deacons were used by God to restrain his evil. They spoke to him and told him to calm down and have a seat. He did as they asked. I was very thankful to God for His common grace in that situation!

After we went back and forth for a couple hours, I simply left them with the gospel. I first explained how we have all broken God's Law in thought, word and deed. Then I explained how Jesus, who is truly God and truly Man, kept the Law for us. He died on the cross taking the wrath of God that we deserved and rose from the dead three days later. And that if we would repent and believe in Him, NOT our works, that we would be saved. His sweet wife gave me a hug on our way out. I think she felt bad for the way her husband acted.

When God Let's Go

Come to find out, in God's amazing providence, Dr. James White debated Jose Ventilacion a week later after we met with those men. Jose Ventilacion is a very well-known debater for the people of Iglesia ni Cristo. Those men that we met with were aware of the debate that was going to happen and said they planned on having their whole church gather at someone's home to watch it. I was so excited when I heard that! It was one to watch for sure. The people in that cult are known for getting violent so looking back now, it makes sense why the man got so upset with me. I thanked the Lord for restraining this man's evil while being in his home.[9]

The flip side to God's common grace of restraining evil is when He stops restraining it. That is when He gives people over to their own wicked desires. When that happens, all hell breaks loose. I believe we have seen some of that in our own country the past 10 years, 2015-2025. The LG-BTQ+ movement has exploded. It is almost like God's restraining hand has been lifted. Most people see all the evil associated with that kind of wickedness and say things like, "This is going to bring the Judgement of God upon us." I don't disagree, because all sin will bring the Judgement of God but in this case what we have been seeing IS the Judgement of God.

Romans 1:18-32 clearly says that, "For the wrath of God is revealed from heaven against all ungodliness and unrighteousness of men, who suppress the truth in unrighteousness, because what may be known of God is manifest in them, for God has shown it to them. For since the

9. James R. White and Jose Ventilacion, "Debate: Who is God?," debate, San Diego, CA, April 24, 2017, https://youtu.be/YEBKNhjNxpY?si=azAAaFxAeVcz-AZH

creation of the world His invisible attributes are clearly seen, being understood by the things that are made, even His eternal power and Godhead, so that they are without excuse, because, although they knew God, they did not glorify Him as God, nor were thankful, but became futile in their thoughts, and their foolish hearts were darkened. Professing to be wise, they became fools, and changed the glory of the incorruptible God into an image made like corruptible man—and birds and four-footed animals and creeping things. THEREFORE God also gave them up to uncleanness, in the lusts of their hearts, to dishonor their bodies among themselves, who exchanged the truth of God for the lie, and worshiped and served the creature rather than the Creator, who is blessed forever. Amen. FOR THIS REASON God gave them up to vile passions. For even their women exchanged the natural use for what is against nature. Likewise also the men, leaving the natural use of the woman, burned in their lust for one another, men with men committing what is shameful, and receiving in themselves the penalty of their error which was due. And even as they did not like to retain God in their knowledge, God gave them over to a debased mind, to do those things which are not fitting; being filled with all unrighteousness, sexual immorality, wickedness, covetousness, maliciousness; full of envy, murder, strife, deceit, evil-mindedness; they are whisperers, backbiters, haters of God, violent, proud, boasters, inventors of evil things, disobedient to parents, undiscerning, untrustworthy, unloving, unforgiving, unmerciful; who, knowing the righteous judgment of God, that those who practice such things are deserving of death, not only do the same but also approve of those who practice them."[10]

The Telos of Common Grace

So as a Christian, I pray and thank God for his common grace! I believe that is what God wants us to pray for. 1 Timothy 2:1-2 says, "Therefore I exhort first of all that supplications, prayer, intercessions, and giving of thanks be made for all men, for kings and all who are in authority, that we may lead a quiet and peaceable life in all godliness and reverence."[11]

Why should we pray for God's common grace? Is it for selfish reasons such as my own comfort and peace? Is it so I can be left alone and not bothered? Not at all. Let's continue reading, "For this is good and acceptable in

10. Romans 1:18-32 (New King James Version).
11. 1 Timothy 2:1-2 (New King James Version).

the sight of God our Savior, who desires all men to be saved and to come to the knowledge of the truth."[12] That is why! The point of common grace is for the salvation of sinners! All kinds of sinners, from kings to presidents to those in positions of authority. Paul said, "Therefore I endure all things for the sake of the elect, that they also may obtain the salvation which is in Christ Jesus with eternal glory."[13]

How will that happen? I'm glad you asked. Let's keep reading and find out. "For there is one God and one Mediator between God and men, the Man Christ Jesus, who gave Himself a ransom for all, to be testified in due time, for which I was appointed a preacher and apostle—I am speaking the truth in Christ and not lying—a teacher of the Gentiles in faith and truth."[14] Common grace is for the preservation of God's creation in order for God to save all of His elect! It is for the glory of God! 1 Timothy 4:10 says, "For to this *end* we both labor and suffer reproach, because we trust in the living God, who is *the* Savior of all men, especially of those who believe." You might be saying to yourself, "That's not fair that God gives common grace to all but only saving grace to His elect?" You are right my friend. That's not fair. That is pure grace! Kind of like how you have a special love for your spouse that you don't have for others.

Thankfulness for Common Grace

So, the next time you are out and about in the marketplace with sinners, give thanks to the God of grace for restraining their evil. But don't forget to thank Him for restraining YOURS as well. He truly is a gracious God! He put a rainbow in the sky to remind you of that precious promise of His common grace to ALL. Worship Him!

"Immediately I was in the Spirit; and behold, a throne set in heaven, and One sat on the throne. And He who sat there was like a jasper and a sardius stone in appearance; and there was a *rainbow* around the throne, in appearance like an emerald. . .they do not rest day or night, saying: 'Holy, holy, holy, Lord God Almighty, Who was and is and is to come!' Whenever the living creatures give glory and honor and thanks to Him who sits on the throne, who lives forever and ever, the twenty-four elders fall down before Him who sits on the throne and worship Him who lives forever and ever,

12. 1 Timothy 2:3-4 (New King James Version).
13. 2 Timothy 2:10 (New King James Version).
14. 1 Timothy 2:5-7 (New King James Version).

and cast their crowns before the throne, saying: 'You are worthy, O Lord, To receive glory and honor and power; For You created all things, and by Your will they exist and were created.'"[15]

---

15. Revelation 4:2-3, 8-11 (New King James Version).

Depth of Mercy! Can There Be
Words by Charles Wesley, 1740

Depth of mercy! Can there be
Mercy still reserved for me?
Can my God His wrath forbear,
Me, the chief of sinners, spare?

I have long withstood His grace,
Long provoked Him to His face,
Would not hearken to His calls,
Grieved Him by a thousand falls.

Whence to me this waste of love?
Ask my Advocate above!
See the cause in Jesus' face,
Now before the throne of grace.

There for me the Savior stands,
Shows His wounds and spreads His hands;
God is love! I know, I feel;
Jesus weeps, and loves me still.[16]

---

16. Charles Wesley, "Depth of Mercy! Can There Be," in *Hymns and Sacred Poems* (London: Strahan, 1740), 59–61

Chapter 12

Fattened for the Slaughter

"You have lived on the earth in pleasure and luxury; you have fattened your hearts as in a day of slaughter." James 5:5[1]

Reason Rally

IN THE SUMMER OF 2016, there was an event that took place in Washington D.C. called the Reason Rally. It was a gathering of atheists who talked about how much they hate the God of the Bible while denying His existence at the same time. . . Reminds me of Romans 1:22, "Professing to be wise, they became fools."[2] Anyways, it was great how the Lord gathered so many lost people together in one place so Christians could share the gospel with them. So, we went! My wife, myself and about 20 other Christians from our Church in Virginia Beach drove up for the event. We met up with the Living Waters team and they gave us bags of books and tracts to pass out. It was an incredible time!

I had one encounter I will never forget. My wife and I were in a spot handing out books and tracts as people walked by. A younger guy, in his twenties, stopped to talk with us. He was riding his bicycle. We had a pretty long conversation, maybe about thirty minutes. He said he used to be a Christian and followed Ray Comfort and Todd Friel, both of whom taught me so much, but was now an atheist. After doing my best to reason with

1. James 5:5 (New King James Version).
2. Romans 1:22 (New King James Version).

him about the Law and the Gospel I realized he was not reasonable at all. I thought we were at a "reason" rally after all. . .

He not only hated the truth, but he hated those who loved him enough to share it with him. Keith Green once said, "I'd rather have people hate me with the knowledge that I tried to save them."[3]

So I thanked him for stopping and talking with us and said, "I have a gift for you."

He laughed and said, "Is it a picture of Ray Comfort with a big brain?"

I said, "No" and handed him a "Gift For You" gospel tract with a 5-dollar bill inside. Those are my favorite to give people after I have shared the gospel with them. There is a slot inside to put real money in, and it has the gospel in it as well. He took the tract with the money in it from me and as he opened it up, he became enraged. He realized there was real money in it. He threw the tract with the money back at me and started yelling and cursing at me. He flipped me off and rode away. It was one of the saddest endings to a witnessing encounter I have ever had.

Glory in Mercy and Judgement

I share that story to say there is another side of the coin of why good things happen to bad people. What about the bad people who do not become Christians, why do good things happen to them? Job 21:7-15 says, "Why do the wicked live and become old, yes, become mighty in power? Their descendants are established with them in their sight, and their offspring before their eyes. Their houses are safe from fear, neither is the rod of God upon them. Their bull breeds without failure; Their cow calves without miscarriage. They send forth their little ones like a flock, and their children dance. They sing to the tambourine and harp, and rejoice to the sound of the flute. They spend their days in wealth, and in a moment go down to the grave. Yet they say to God, 'Depart from us, for we do not desire the knowledge of Your ways. Who is the Almighty, that we should serve Him? And what profit do we have if we pray to Him?'"[4]

The reason good things happen to wicked people who never repent and trust in Christ is for the glory of God. See, God is glorified when He saves a sinner. His mercy, grace and love are put on display through their

3. Ray Comfort, ed., *The Evidence Study Bible: New King James Version* (Alachua, FL: Bridge-Logos Publishers, 2011), 242, quoting Keith Green.
4. Job 21:7-15 (New King James Version).

salvation which brings Him much glory. But what about when they die in their sins? How does that glorify God? In that scenario God's wrath, holiness and justice are seen clearly which also gives Him glory.

I remember thinking about why God created the world the way He did. After all, He is God and can do whatever He wants. Why not create a world where everyone goes to heaven? Why not a world where everyone goes to hell? Why the world in which we live where some go to heaven and some go to hell? Answer: For His glory! God created the world in which we live and everything in it to put HIMSELF on display!

Romans 9:22,23 says, "What if God, wanting to show His wrath and to make His power known endured with much longsuffering the vessels of wrath prepared for destruction, and that He might make known the riches of His glory on the vessels of mercy which He had prepared beforehand for glory."[5] You see, if everyone went to hell then we would never know of His grace, mercy and love. If everyone went to heaven, we would not know anything about his wrath and justice. But in the world He created and especially at the cross, where Jesus died, we see ALL His perfections on display! On the cross we see His holiness, righteousness, justice and wrath being poured out on His Son for sinners. But we also see His love, mercy and grace for His people as Christ bore our sins in His body on the tree![6] While I delve into this topic, I first want to bring to mind a couple passages of Scripture. Firstly, God takes no pleasure in the death of the wicked. Ezekiel 33:11 says, "Say to them: 'As I live,' says the Lord God, 'I have no pleasure in the death of the wicked, but that the wicked turn from his way and live. Turn, turn from your evil ways! For why should you die, O house of Israel?'"[7]

Vessels of Wrath

At the same time God does raise up men and women throughout the Bible and history who have been very wicked. Take Pharoah for example. He was rich and powerful and enslaved God's people for over 400 years. Why? God tells us why in Romans 9:17 which says, "For the Scripture says to Pharaoh, 'For this very purpose I have raised you up, that I may show

---

5. Romans 9:22-23 (New King James Version).

6. 1 Peter 2:24 (New King James Version).

7. Ezekiel 33:11 (New King James Version).

My power in you, and that My name may be declared in all the earth.'"[8] Pharaoh was being "fattened for the slaughter." Every person breathes because God puts breath in their lungs. They enjoy sunsets because God gives them eyes to see with. They love the smell of bacon because God gives them a nose to smell with. They enjoy good music because God gives them ears to hear with. Instead of thanking God and worshiping Him, they hate God and worship themselves.

God has lavished His goodness upon all mankind. Mankind in his rebellion uses those blessings not to praise God but to wage war against Him. So, what looks like prosperity so much of the time turns out to be a fattening for the slaughter. Those who refuse to bend the knee to King Jesus are storing up wrath for the day of Judgement. Romans 2:5 says, "But in accordance with your hardness and your impenitent heart you are treasuring up for yourself wrath in the day of wrath and revelation of the righteous judgement of God."[9]

We don't know who will ultimately end up being fattened for the slaughter, like Pharoah, or who will end up being a trophy of grace, like the Apostle Paul. As Christians we continue to pray and plead with them to look to Christ and live! My father and I have had many conversations and debates about Christianity and Islam. We have gone and talked to Imams in the Mosque before. My dad has looked me in the eye and said, "I will never become a Christian. I will die a Muslim." I pray that is not the case.

A Final Plea

My step-daughter Jordan and I have had many conversations about Christ and His Gospel. She was a lesbian when I met her at the age of thirteen, eleven years ago. Shortly after that she claimed to be "transgender." We had lots of talks about that up until about a year ago when she cut her mother and I out of her life because she wanted to marry her girlfriend Morgan and we would not support her or attend the ceremony. I remember one time Jordan and I were at the Ark Encounter in Kentucky and after seeing the amazing ship we went back to the hotel room. We began talking about heaven, hell and the gospel. She looked at me and said words that sent chills through my spine to this very day. She looked me in the eye and said, "I would rather go to hell as a boy than to heaven as a girl." I continue

8. Romans 9:17 (New King James Version).
9. Romans 2:5 (New King James Version).

to pray for her and hope she doesn't get what she deserves. Is that fair? NO, it is grace! I was able to write her a letter a few years ago before she stopped talking to me. Here is what I wrote:

Dear Jordan,

Hello my favorite step-daughter. I miss you lots and hope to see you again soon! Your momma and I pray for you ALL the time. I hope these gifts from us bless you as much as they have us. I got this book for you "Irreversible Damage" after I listened to it on audible. It broke my heart and brought tears to my eyes! I got it for you not because I thought it would "convert" you, only the Gospel can do that, but because as I listened to it I could only think of YOU. You were only thirteen years old when we met and what I listened to provoked a lot of righteous anger towards the people who coached you along the way. You were just a child and are still a young girl. I am so sad and angry. I LOVE YOU! A preacher once said, "Your best friend is the person who tells you the most truth."[10] Remember that, people who truly love and care about you will tell you the truth even if it hurts BECAUSE THEY LOVE YOU. Those who won't don't love you. They actually just love themselves. Well as you know, I do love you and we have had many conversations about the truth. In this letter I want to reiterate some of those truths because I love and care about you. "Open rebuke is better than love carefully concealed. Faithful are the wounds of a friend, but the kisses of an enemy are deceitful." Proverbs 27:5,6.[11] What that means is a true friend will speak truth even if it hurts you while an enemy tells you what YOU want to hear which is deceitful. The truth is that God is our Creator. Genesis 1:27 says, "So God created man in His own image; in the image of God He created him; male and female He created them."[12] God made me a male and you a female and that is a GOOD thing. I remember a statement you made to me once that broke my heart. You said, "I would rather go to hell as a boy than to heaven as a girl." To be honest Jordan, if you go to heaven or hell you will go there as a girl. That is your only option. There is no such thing as transitioning. You can grow the biggest beard, have the hairiest legs, get the deepest voice, have your breasts removed, etc. and you will still be a girl because God made you a girl. Just like a guy can wear a dress, put on make-up, castrate themselves, get

10. Author unknown, quoted in The Quotable Christian, ed. Robert J. Morgan (Grand Rapids: Baker Books, 1997), 132.

11. Proverbs 27:5-6 (New King James Version).

12. Genesis 1:27 (New King James Version).

breast implants and yet they will remain a guy because that is how God made them. ANYONE who tells you otherwise is not your friend but is actually an enemy giving you kisses according to Proverbs 27:6. Isaiah 5:20 says, "Woe to those who call evil good, and good evil."[13] The word 'woe' is actually a curse. God is cursing those who call women, men and men, women. People who call you by male pronouns or by a male name or encourage you to rebel against the fact that you are a woman created by God are lying to you. Read Romans chapter 1 sometime.[14] No matter how much the world hates you and continues to encourage you in your sin against God I will never stop speaking the truth to you in love. Repent (turn from your sin to Christ) and trust in Him alone! God made you a female and that is a WONDERFUL thing! Thank Him for that! Praise Him for that! He is GOOD! This life is short and will be over SOON! Charles Spurgeon, the prince of preachers, once asked, "Is sin so luscious that you will burn in hell forever for it?"[15] Please, Jordan! I love you baby girl! You are going to die one day and face a holy God. He is so holy, Jordan, that He considers lust to be adultery and hatred murder. He says lying lips are an abomination and that all liars will have their part in the lake of fire. God is a consuming fire! It is a fearful thing to fall into the hands of the living God! Hell is FOREVER. Jesus said in Luke 12:4-5, "And I say to you, My friends, do not be afraid of those who kill the body, and after that have no more that they can do. But I will show you whom you should fear: Fear Him who, after He has killed, has power to cast into hell; yes, I say to you fear Him!"[16] Listen to Christ, Jordan! Fear God! Flee from your sin that will only bring you misery, death and hell. Run to the One who is Eternal Life Himself! He loves to save sinners! He loves saving the worst of sinners!! Look at ME! I am the worst of sinners and He has saved me. What a kind God He is. He is rich in mercy to ALL who call upon Him in TRUTH! That is what Christmas is ALL about. God became a Man. Jesus is truly God and truly Man. He kept God's Law perfectly. He never sinned once. Then He went to the cross to suffer and die taking the wrath of God sinners deserve. 3 days later He rose from the grave defeating DEATH! That is good news for all who repent and believe! And yet it is the most terrifying news for those who will not. Spurgeon said, "The most terrible warning to impenitent men

13. Isaiah 5:20 (New King James Version).

14. Romans 1:1-32 (New King James Version).

15. Ray Comfort, ed., *The Evidence Study Bible: New King James Version* (Alachua, FL: Bridge-Logos Publishers, 2011), 885, quoting Charles Spurgeon.

16. Luke 12:4-5 (New King James Version).

in all the world is the death of Christ. For if God spared not His only Son, on whom was only laid imputed sin, will He spare sinners whose sins are their own?"[17] Turn to Him NOW! "Behold, now is the accepted time; behold, now is the day of salvation." 2 Cor. 6:2.[18]

17. Ray Comfort, ed., *The Evidence Study Bible: New King James Version* (Alachua, FL: Bridge-Logos Publishers, 2011), 1803, quoting Charles Spurgeon.

18. 2 Corinthians 6:2 (New King James Version).

Ye Wretched, Hungry, Starving Poor
Words by Anne Steele, 1760

Ye wretched, hungry, starving poor,
Behold a royal feast!
Where mercy spreads her bounteous store,
For every humble guest.

Come to the living waters, come!
Sinners, obey your Lord:
Return, ye weary wand'rers, home,
And find His gracious word.

See from the Rock a fountain rise!
For you in healing streams;
The desert shall with plenty flow,
And light restore your dreams.

O come, ye sinners, to your Lord,
In Christ to paradise restored;
His proffered benefits embrace,
The plenitude of gospel grace.[19]

19. Anne Steele, "Ye Wretched, Hungry, Starving Poor," in *Poems on Subjects Chiefly Devotional*, vol. 1 (London: J. Buckland, 1760), 134–35.

Chapter 13

Do You Have Beautiful Feet?

"How beautiful upon the mountains are the feet of him who brings good news, who proclaims peace, who brings glad tidings of good *things,* who proclaims salvation, who says to Zion, "Your God reigns!""[1]

Rebuked by an Atheist

I HAVE ALWAYS LOVED to watch magicians. One of my favorite shows is called Penn & Teller: Fool Us. Penn and Teller are magicians who have other magicians come on their show hoping to fool them. If they perform their act without either Penn or Teller figuring out how they did it, they get a trophy. One of the hosts, Penn Jillette, is a well-known atheist. I have heard it said before that he hates God so much that he crosses out the word 'God' off every dollar bill he touches. He also, supposedly, has the letters 'dog on' on his license plate, which spelt backwards says, 'no god.' So, he is a committed militant atheist to say the least. There is a YouTube video where Penn tells of a businessman who approached him after one of his shows and gave him a Bible. Here is a snippet of what he said in the video.

"It was really wonderful. I believe he knew that I was an atheist, but he was not defensive, and he looked me right in the eyes. . .and then gave me this Bible. I've always said that I don't respect people who don't proselytize. I don't respect that at all. If you believe that there's a heaven and hell, and

1. Isaiah 52:7 (New King James Version).

people could be going to hell, or not getting eternal life, or whatever, and you think that, 'Well, it's not really worth telling them this because it would make it socially awkward'—HOW MUCH DO YOU HAVE TO HATE SOMEBODY TO BELIEVE THAT EVERLASTING LIFE IS POSSIBLE AND NOT TELL THEM THAT? I mean if I believed beyond a shadow of a doubt that a truck was coming at you, and you didn't believe it, and that truck was bearing down on you, there is a certain point where I would tackle you—and this is more important than that. . .He cared enough about me to proselytize and give me a Bible."[2]

I couldn't have said it any better myself. As soon as God saved me, I immediately got a concern for the lost and not just my immediate family that was lost but for ALL people. Even unbelievers don't want their family to go to hell, just ask the rich man in Luke 16.[3] I was lost and had been found. I was blind and could now see. I have always been troubled by professing Christians who are apathetic when it comes to evangelism. Charles Spurgeon once said, "Have you no wish for others to be saved, then you are not saved yourself, be sure of that!"[4] Jesus said, "Follow Me, and I will make you become fishers of men."[5] Christ did not say He would TRY to make men become fishers or that He MIGHT but rather that he WILL make men fishers of men. If you are not fishing, you are not following said one theologian.

Sadly, in my experience a concern for the lost with a willingness to share the gospel with them is not a high priority among many professing Christians today. Jesus' words to His disciples are just as relevant now as they were when He spoke them 2,000 years ago, "The harvest truly *is* plentiful, but the laborers *are* few. Therefore pray the Lord of the harvest to send out laborers into His harvest." (Matthew 9:37-38)[6] Ray Comfort commenting on this verse said, "If we are not laborers, we won't obey this command, because our conscience will condemn us. The devil therefore

2. Jillette, Penn. "A Gift of a Bible." YouTube video, 5:11. Posted by "beinzee," July 8, 2010. https://youtu.be/6md638smQd8?si=h_WiA2IcghHaxaOg

3. Luke 16:19-31 (New King James Version).

4. Ray Comfort, ed., *The Evidence Study Bible: New King James Version* (Alachua, FL: Bridge-Logos Publishers, 2011), s.v. "Charles Spurgeon," quoting Charles Spurgeon.

5. Mark 1:17 (New King James Version).

6. Matthew 9:37-38 (New King James Version).

gets two victories: not only does the professing Christian not labor in the harvest fields, but neither does he pray for laborers."[7]

Free Water

During the summer months back in Virginia Beach, my wife and I had a group of about 10-12 people who would go out on Saturdays to witness. We would have a couple coolers full of ice and bottles of water along with a backpack full of tracts with a book by Jonny Mac, as we liked to say. We would pray together as a group for God's help and then we would spread out up and down the boardwalk in groups of 2 or 3. As people walked by, we would hold out the tracts and say, "How y'all doing today? Did you get one of these?"

As they would reach out to grab the tract I would follow with, "Would you like some free water?" It was a great way to get people to stop.

They would say, "Sure, I'll take a water."

As I would get them water, I would ask them where they were from and then I would ask them THE question of questions. . . "What do you believe happens after we die?"

The Lord was always so kind to us. We had so many fruitful conversations with lost people with that approach. We would get to hold up the mirror of God's Law and then show them how that points us all to Christ for cleansing. To be honest, no matter how the person responded, it was ALWAYS a success. Isaiah 55:10,11 says, "For as the rain comes down, and the snow from heaven, and do not return there, but water the earth, and make it bring forth and bud, that it may give seed to the sower and bread to the eater, so shall My word be that goes forth from My mouth; It shall not return to Me void, but it shall accomplish what I please, and it shall prosper in the thing for which I sent it."[8]

Every time we went out with the gospel some would reject it, some might receive it, and others would have more questions. It reminded me of when Paul preached his famous sermon on Mars Hill in Acts 17. At the end of his sermon this is what is recorded in verses 32-34, "And when they heard of the resurrection of the dead, some mocked, while others said, 'We will hear you again on this matter.' So Paul departed from among them.

7. Ray Comfort, ed., *The Evidence Study Bible: New King James Version* (Alachua, FL: Bridge-Logos Publishers, 2011), 1343, comment on Matthew 9:38.

8. Isaiah 55:10-11 (New King James Version).

However, some men joined him and believed, among them Dionysius the Areopagite, a woman named Damaris, and others with them."[9] The greatest failure of evangelism today is when we fail to evangelize. "Therefore, my beloved brethren, be steadfast, immovable, always abounding in the work of the Lord, knowing that your labor is not in vain in the Lord." 1 Corinthians 15:58.[10]

One summer weekend a few of us went out to witness at the oceanfront in Virginia Beach. Billy, an older gentleman from my church, and I were on the sidewalk talking with people. A younger couple walked by and stopped for some water. I gave them each a water and a tract and asked where they were from.

They said, "Las Vegas." We had a great conversation. After walking them through the Law and Gospel the woman said something like, "I have never heard it explained that way before. That makes a lot of sense." I pleaded with them both to repent and believe in the gospel.

As I thanked them for the conversation and gave them some literature, the woman looked me in the eyes and said, "I am so glad we stopped for a bottle of water." I thought to myself, we are not just giving people bottles of water to quench their thirst for a moment, but we are giving them Living Water that would quench their thirst FOREVER! "Jesus answered and said to her, 'Whoever drinks of this water will thirst again, but whoever drinks of the water that I shall give him will never thirst. But the water that I shall give him will become in him a fountain of water springing up into everlasting life'" John 4:13,14.[11]

A Waitress Encounters the Gospel

Another encounter that was so encouraging was at Buffalo Wild Wings. I used to live there back in the day. I would always go either on Tuesdays, Thursdays or whenever there was a UFC fight. I have been able to have so many conversations with the servers while having a meal with a brother or two from Church. This one day was pretty special. One of the professors from a seminary in Virginia Beach and I met at Buffalo Wild Wings to have lunch. Shortly after we sat down our waitress came out to introduce herself and asked us what we would like to drink. After we ordered our food, we

9. Acts 17:32-34 (New King James Version).
10. 1 Corinthians 15:58 (New King James Version).
11. John 4:13-14 (New King James Version).

told her that we were going to pray for our food and asked her how we could pray for her. She was taken aback and asked if we would pray for her as she was taking classes at Tidewater Community College. I asked her what she was going to school for. She replied, "Psychology for children." So, after she walked off, we prayed for our meal, for her school and for her soul.

After we prayed and got our food we were able to talk with her more. I asked her why she wanted to be a psychologist for children. She told me that she had children and wanted to understand why they act the way they do. I was so excited when I heard that. I immediately asked her if she thought children were born good or evil. She said what I expected her to say, "Good."

So, I quickly asked her about her children, I said, "So did you teach your children to be bad? Did you teach them to lie and hit each other or be selfish?"

She got a big grin on her face and said, "No." She said, "I guess they do those things naturally."

I said, "Yep. That is their nature. They are born with a sinful nature."

She nodded in agreement and so I asked her, "Would you consider yourself to be a good person?"

She said, "Yes." I then proceeded with God's Holy Law to show how she truly measured up to God's standard.

After taking her through the 10 Commandments to show her that only God is good, I followed that with the glorious gospel of Christ. Her whole complexion changed as we talked. She was humbled by the Law and then her face lit up as I shared with her the good news of how God loves sinners so much that He gave His only begotten Son that whoever believes in Him will not perish but will have everlasting life.[12] We gave her some Christian literature for her to read and left her with a generous tip. Before we left, she came over and said, "I needed to hear this. Thank you so much for sharing that with me. Would it be okay for me to give you a hug?" I smiled and said, "Of course!" I stood up and gave her a hug and we left the restaurant rejoicing and leaping with joy!

Those encounters are so encouraging and exciting! I believe we experienced repentance right before our eyes as she placed her faith in Christ alone. All of heaven was rejoicing in that moment! Luke 15:5-10 says, "What man of you, having a hundred sheep, if he loses one of them, does not leave the ninety-nine in the wilderness, and go after the one

12. John 3:16 (New King James Version).

which is lost until he finds it? And when he has found it, he lays it on his shoulders, rejoicing. And when he comes home, he calls together his friends and neighbors, saying to them, 'Rejoice with me, for I have found my sheep which was lost!' I say to you that likewise there will be more joy in heaven over one sinner who repents than over ninety-nine just persons who need no repentance. Or what woman, having ten silver coins, if she loses one coin, does not light a lamp, sweep the house, and search carefully until she finds it? And when she has found it, she calls her friends and neighbors together, saying, 'Rejoice with me, for I have found the piece which I lost!' Likewise, I say to you, there is joy in the presence of the angels of God over one sinner who repents."[13]

Vessels for Honor

I don't know about you but if there is one thing that motivates me regarding evangelism, it is knowing what God the Father rejoices about in heaven! Since He rejoices over sinners who repent, I want to see as many people as I can repent and believe in the gospel. I also desire greatly to be a vessel that God uses to make that happen. That can only happen if we open our mouths and proclaim the everlasting gospel to lost souls! "Therefore if anyone cleanses himself from the latter, he will be a vessel for honor, sanctified and useful for the Master, prepared for every good work." 2 Timothy 2:21.[14] I cannot think of a better good work, can you?

By God's grace and God's grace alone I have had many wonderful witnessing encounters. Every time I go anywhere, I pray that the Lord would use me to reach the lost. He answers my prayer every time! If I don't get to have a conversation, I at least am able to give them a tract. If I don't give out a tract, I am able to leave one somewhere. Credit card slots at gas pumps are great places to leave them or empty plastic grocery bags at the stores. There are so many places to leave tracts so people may pick them up and read them. Tracts are a wonderful way to get the gospel out. The Apostle Paul said, "I have become all things to all men, that I might by ALL MEANS save some." 1 Corinthians 9:22.[15]

The great open-air preacher George Whitefield read a gospel tract called *The Life of God in the Soul of a Man*. After reading it he said, "God

13. Luke 15:5-10 (New King James Version).

14. 2 Timothy 2:21 (New King James Version).

15. 1 Corinthians 9:22 (New King James Version).

showed me I must be born again or be damned." He went on to pray, "Lord, if I am not a Christian, or if I am not a real one, for Jesus Christ's sake show me what Christianity is, that I may not be damned at last!" Then he wrote in his journal "from that moment. . .did I know that I must become a new creature."[16] God used a gospel tract to save Hudson Taylor the great missionary to China.

Charles Spurgeon, the prince of preachers, once said, "When preaching and private talk are not available, you need to have a tract ready. . .Get good striking tracts, or none at all. But a touching gospel tract may be the seed of eternal life. Therefore, do not go out without your tracts."[17]

Calling All Men

If God can use a weak, wretched, vile sinner like myself, He can use ANY-BODY! God took Peter the fisherman and made him a fisher of men. He took Paul the tent maker and turned him into one who makes "tents" fit for heaven! He also saved me when I was a firefighter and has now called me to "save with fear, *pulling them out of the fire*, hating even the garment defiled by the flesh" (Jude 23). Go to Him and cry out for His strength, for His wisdom, for His boldness and He will give it to you above and beyond anything you can think or imagine. "Now to Him who is able to do exceedingly abundantly above all that we ask or think, according to the power that works in us, to Him be glory in the church by Christ Jesus to all generations, forever and ever. Amen."[18]

Let your fears and weaknesses be your strengths. Let us imitate Paul in this manner where he said, "And I, brethren, when I came to you, did not come with excellence of speech or of wisdom declaring to you the testimony of God. For I determined not to know anything among you except Jesus Christ and Him crucified. I was with you in weakness, in fear, and in much trembling. And my speech and my preaching were not with persuasive words of human wisdom, but in demonstration of the Spirit

16. Ray Comfort, ed., *The Evidence Study Bible: New King James Version* (Alachua, FL: Bridge-Logos Publishers, 2011), 1644, quoting George Whitefield.

17. Ray Comfort, ed., *The Evidence Study Bible: New King James Version* (Alachua, FL: Bridge-Logos Publishers, 2011), 1644, quoting Charles Spurgeon.

18. Ephesians 3:20 (New King James Version).

and of power, that your faith should not be in the wisdom of men but in the power of God."[19]

This is why you were created, to know God and to make Him known. Luke 19:10 says, "For the Son of Man came to seek and save that which is lost."[20] This is our purpose on earth! John MacArthur said, "If God's primary purpose for the saved were loving fellowship, He would take believers immediately to heaven, where spiritual fellowship is perfect, unhindered by sin, disharmony, or loneliness. If His primary purpose for the saved were the learning of His Word, He would also take believers immediately to heaven, where His Word is perfectly known and understood. And if God's primary purpose for the saved were to give Him praise, He would, again, take believers immediately to heaven, where praise is perfect and unending. There is only one reason the Lord allows His Church to remain on earth: to seek and save the lost, just as Christ's only reason for coming to earth was to seek and to save the lost. 'As the Father has sent Me,' He declared, 'I also send you' (John 20:21). Therefore, believers who are not committed to winning the lost for Jesus Christ should reexamine their relationship to the Lord and certainly their divine reason for existence. Fellowship, teaching, and praise are not the mission of the Church but are rather the preparation of the Church to fulfill its mission of winning the lost. And just as in athletics, training should never be confused with or substituted for actually competing in the game, which is the reason for all the training."[21]

Stirred for Zeal

I pray that the Lord will stir your heart for this great irksome task of evangelism. Study men like David Brainard, George Whitefield, Charles Spurgeon and Ray Comfort for starters. If you are not greatly encouraged by this calling that all believers have, you must repent of your apathy and run to the Lord Jesus Christ for mercy and grace. He will pour it out on you GENEROUSLY. Is that fair? No, it is grace! May God give us all a greater zeal for His name and for lost souls. Zeal is lacking in all of us to one degree or another. Charles Spurgeon said regarding zeal, "If you never have sleepless hours, if you never have weeping eyes, if your hearts never

19. 1 Corinthians 2:1-5 (New King James Version).

20. Luke 19:10 (New King James Version).

21. Ray Comfort, ed., *The Evidence Study Bible: New King James Version* (Alachua, FL: Bridge-Logos Publishers, 2011), 1471, quoting John MacArthur.

swell as if they would burst, you need not anticipate that you will be called zealous. You do not know the beginning of true zeal, for the foundation of Christian zeal lies in the heart. The heart must be heavy with grief and yet must beat high with holy ardor. The heart must be vehement in desire, panting continually for God's glory, or else we shall never attain to anything like the zeal which God would have us know."[22]

Jesus said, "Come to Me, all you who labor and are heavy laden, and I will give you rest."[23] THAT is our message to the world, bride of Christ! We tell them to COME! Rev. 22:17 says, "And the Spirit and the bride say, 'COME!' And let him who hears say, 'COME!' And let him who thirsts COME! Whoever desires, let him take the water of life freely."[24]

"Now may the God of peace who brought up our Lord Jesus from the dead, that great Shepherd of the sheep, through the blood of the everlasting covenant make you complete in every good work to do His will, working in you what is well pleasing in His sight, through Jesus Christ, to whom be glory forever and ever. Amen." Hebrews 13:20,21.[25]

22. Ray Comfort, ed., *The Evidence Study Bible: New King James Version* (Alachua, FL: Bridge-Logos Publishers, 2011), 1669, quoting Charles Spurgeon.

23. Matthew 11:28 (New King James Version).

24. Revelation 22:17 (New King James Version).

25. Hebrews 13:20-21 (New King James Version).

My Friend
Anonymous

My friend, I stand in judgment now,
and feel that you're to blame somehow.
On earth I walked with you by day,
and never did you show the way.

You knew the Savior in truth and glory,
But never did you tell the story.
My knowledge then was very dim.
You could have led me safe to Him.

Though we lived together, here on earth,
you never told me of the second birth.
and now I stand before eternal hell,
because of heaven's glory you did not tell![26]

---

26. Ray Comfort, ed., *The Evidence Study Bible: New King James Version* (Alachua, FL: Bridge-Logos Publishers, 2011), 1711.

Chapter 14

There is Only One Hero

"This is My beloved Son, in whom I am well pleased. Hear Him!"[1]

66 Books: One Christ

ONE OF MY FAVORITE questions to ask people is what the Bible is about. I have heard many different answers to that question. Some say it is a book of rules and principles for life. Others may say it is a book about history. Some say it is a collection of stories and lessons. Others might say it is a book of mythology or allegory. The number one rule of hermeneutics, the art and science of interpreting scripture, is the analogy of faith (Scripture interprets Scripture). Or as some have said, the best commentary on the Holy Spirit is the Holy Spirit. So, to answer the question, let's go to the Book itself.

Jesus was in a debate with the religious leaders of His day in John chapter 5. He was giving a defense of Himself using witnesses like Deuteronomy 19:15 called for: "One witness shall not rise against a man concerning any iniquity or any sin that he commits; by the mouth of two or three witnesses the matter shall be established."[2] In the midst of His defense He says something that would have made you pick up stones to stone Him, if it wasn't true. In John 5:39 Jesus says this, "You search the Scriptures, for in them you think you have eternal life; but these are they which testify of

1. Matthew 17:6 (New King James Version).
2. Deuteronomy 19:15 (New King James Version).

Me."[3] Wow! Here is the answer to our question. Jesus says the whole Bible is about HIM! With that truth in mind when we go back to the Old Testament, it sheds light on everything we read.

Adam's Fall Brings A Savior for All

When God created Adam, He made a covenant with him called the covenant of works. He was given a mandate to take dominion, be fruitful and multiply and work the garden. Just as God worked six days and rested on the seventh, so Adam was to complete the work God had given him and then he would have entered into God's rest. As we know from Genesis 3, Adam fell. He disobeyed God and ate from the tree God forbid him to. Adam is the Federal Head of all of humanity. That simply means he is our representative. When Adam fell in the garden, the rest of us fell in him. "For as in Adam all die." 1 Cor. 15:22.[4] What that means is we are all born sinners. Before you get upset with Adam because he fell as our representative, just know that you would have fallen faster. He was the best representative for humanity!

After Adam fell, he realized he was naked and hid from God, which is funny when you think about it. How can you hide from God? That is what sin does to you. As one preacher said before, "Sin makes you stupid." So, the LORD finds Adam and as He is laying out the consequences for sin, what He says to the serpent in Genesis 3:15 gives us a glimmer of hope. Genesis 3:15, also known as the Protoevangelium, the first gospel, says, "And I will put enmity between you and the woman, and between your seed and her Seed; He shall bruise your head, and you shall bruise His heel."[5] The rest of Scripture is a footnote to that verse! As you read from Genesis to Malachi you should read with great anticipation looking for the Seed who will crush the head of the serpent.

A Few Good Men, No Not One

As we look briefly at Genesis, we can see the anticipation for the Seed but also the utter failure of men to fulfill that promise. Let's look at Noah for

3. John 5:39 (New King James Version).
4. 1 Corinthians 15:22 (New King James Version).
5. Genesis 3:15 (New King James Version).

example. Genesis 5:28,29 says, "Lamech lived one hundred and eighty-two years, and had a son. And he called his name Noah, saying, "This one will comfort us concerning our work and the toil of our hands, because of the ground which the Lord has cursed."[6] So as you read it you should be saying, "Is this the promised seed from Genesis 3:15 who will crush the head of the serpent?" As we keep reading in Genesis, we get to Genesis 9 after the flood and we read this about Noah, "So God blessed Noah and his sons, and said to them: "Be fruitful and multiply, and fill the earth."[7] This sounds promising doesn't it? God is giving the same mandate to Noah that He gave to Adam with one exception, no dominion mandate.

After God made the covenant with Noah and all creation, commonly referred to as the Noahic Covenant, something tragic happens. Genesis 9:20-23 gives us the account: "Noah began to be a farmer, and he planted a vineyard. Then he drank of the wine and was drunk, and became uncovered in his tent. And Ham, the father of Canaan, saw the nakedness of his father, and told his two brothers outside. But Shem and Japheth took a garment, laid it on both their shoulders, and went backward and covered the nakedness of their father. Their faces were turned away, and they did not see their father's nakedness."[8]

Our anticipation of, "Could this be the one" turned into an unfortunate NOPE. Just as Adam ate fruit from the garden he wasn't supposed to and ended up naked and ashamed, Noah, his great-great-great-great-great-great-great-great-grandson followed in his great^8 grandpa's footsteps. He also ate from the fruit of the vine and ended up naked and ashamed. Both of their nakedness had to be covered by another.

We then come to Abram who is later renamed Abraham. As we read his story we might be thinking, is he the promised one? Then as we keep reading, we hear about his encounter with Pharaoh in Genesis 12:10-20: "Now there was a famine in the land, and Abram went down to Egypt to dwell there, for the famine was severe in the land. And it came to pass, when he was close to entering Egypt, that he said to Sarai his wife, "Indeed I know that you are a woman of beautiful countenance. Therefore it will happen, when the Egyptians see you, that they will say, 'This is his wife'; and they will kill me, but they will let you live. Please say you are my sister, that it may be well with me for your sake, and that I may live because of you." So it was,

---

6. Genesis 5:28-29 (New King James Version).

7. Genesis 9:1 (New King James Version).

8. Genesis 9:20-23 (New King James Version).

when Abram came into Egypt, that the Egyptians saw the woman, that she was very beautiful. The princes of Pharaoh also saw her and commended her to Pharaoh. And the woman was taken to Pharaoh's house. He treated Abram well for her sake. He had sheep, oxen, male donkeys, male and female servants, female donkeys, and camels. But the Lord plagued Pharaoh and his house with great plagues because of Sarai, Abram's wife. And Pharaoh called Abram and said, "What is this you have done to me? Why did you not tell me that she was your wife? Why did you say, 'She is my sister'? I might have taken her as my wife. Now therefore, here is your wife; take her and go your way." So, Pharaoh commanded his men concerning him; and they sent him away, with his wife and all that he had."[9]

Abraham not only lied, but told his wife to lie for him. Why? Because he had a fear of man. Proverbs 29:25 says, "The fear of man brings a snare, but whoever trusts in the Lord shall be safe."[10] Abraham was not trusting in the Lord. He also repeated this same sin later on in Genesis 20 with Abimelech, king of Gerar.[11] Something else interesting is going on in this passage as well as others in Genesis. There is a phrase that is repeated.

When Adam and Eve sinned against God in Genesis 3 God said, "What have you done?"[12] In the next chapter after Cain killed his brother Abel, the Lord said to him, "What have you done?"[13] In Genesis 12 and 20, both accounts where Abraham lied about Sarai being his wife, both rulers said to Abraham, "What is this you have done to me?"[14] Then in Genesis 31 after Jacob deceives Laban, Laban confronts Jacob and says to him, "What have you done?"[15] And if God spoke to you or I today, He would say the exact same thing, "What have you done?"

In Adam All Die

So, what we see happening right away in the book of Genesis after Adam falls is ALL of his offspring are corrupt. ALL OF THEM. Scripture shouts about it everywhere you turn. Let's flip over to the next book in the Bible.

9. Genesis 12:10-20 (New King James Version).

10. Proverbs 29:25 (New King James Version).

11. Genesis 20:1-18 (New King James Version).

12. Genesis 3:13 (New King James Version).

13. Genesis 4:10 (New King James Version).

14. Genesis 12:18; Genesis 20:9 (New King James Version).

15. Genesis 31:26 (New King James Version).

There we meet a man named Moses. Moses is the great deliverer. There he meets another Pharaoh just like Abraham did back in Genesis. Pharaohs would wear headgear featuring a serpent on it. Surely Moses is the promised one who will crush the head of this serpent that Abraham failed too. Nope. He killed an Egyptian with his bare hands and struck a rock twice in the wilderness when he was supposed to only speak to it. Because of that Moses was not allowed to enter the promised land.[16] Moses represented the Law. D.L. Moody said, "The Law can only chase a man to Calvary, no further."[17]

We could start to read about King David and think "Is he the promised seed?" I mean, he did kill Goliath who was dressed in a coat of scale armor looking like a snake. He crushed his skull with his stone as it sank into his forehead and even cut it off after that. Surely David is the promised seed! I don't think so. . . Remember Bathsheba.[18] What about Samson? His birth was foretold by the Angel of the Lord. He was to be a Nazirite to God from the womb. He was called to deliver Israel out of the hands of the Philistines. He was a Judge of Israel with superhuman strength. Was he the promised head crusher? Nope. His downfall was foreign women, just like Solomon's was.[19]

Christ Alone

Every character in the Bible is tainted with sin except ONE. They are ALL Bad Boys. "For there is not a just man on earth who does good and does not sin." Ecclesiastes 7:20.[20] There is only One Hero in the Bible, the Lord Jesus Christ! After Jesus was crucified in the book of Luke, He rose from the dead three days later. On that same day He met two disciples on the road to Emmaus. He walked with them for seven miles and talked with them about the crucifixion. At the beginning of their conversation, He said this to them, ""O foolish ones, and slow of heart to believe in all that the prophets have spoken! Ought not the Christ to have suffered these things and to enter into His glory?" And beginning at Moses and all the Prophets, He expounded to

16. Exodus 2:11-12; Numbers 20:7-12 (New King James Version).

17. Ray Comfort, ed., *The Evidence Study Bible: New King James Version* (Alachua, FL: Bridge-Logos Publishers, 2011), s.v. "D. L. Moody," quoting D. L. Moody.

18. 2 Samuel 11:1-27 (New King James Version).

19. Judges 16:4-21; 1 Kings 11:1-8 (New King James Version).

20. Ecclesiastes 7:20 (New King James Version).

them in all the Scriptures the things concerning Himself."[21] After the two disciples had that encounter with the risen Christ, they immediately found the other disciples who were gathered together and told them what happened. As they were telling them about what had happened, Jesus Himself stood in the midst of them. After demonstrating that He wasn't a ghost, He said to them, 'These are the words which I spoke to you while I was still with you, that all things must be fulfilled which were written in the Law of Moses and the Prophets and the Psalms concerning Me.'" Luke 24:44.[22] Jesus emphatically declared that the whole Bible is about Him!

The whole Bible is full of bad boys and girls. Every single person in it is corrupted by sin, EVEN Mary, except for The Lord Jesus Christ! He is the sinless, spotless Lamb of God! Christ is holy, harmless, undefiled and separate from sinners! HE is the SEED who crushed the head of the serpent! "Therefore, since the children share in flesh and blood, He Himself likewise also partook of the same, so that through death He might destroy the one who has the power of death, that is, the devil, and free those who through fear of death were subject to slavery all their lives."[23]

The Last Adam

The second Adam came two thousand years ago, born of a woman, born under the Law, to redeem those who were under the Law. Jesus, the last Adam, did what the first Adam failed to do. Christ as perfect God and perfect Man kept God's Law on behalf of His imperfect people. The God-Man took dominion over EVERYTHING and now possesses ALL authority in heaven and on earth! He is the Prophet, Priest and King! He is the greater Temple, the greater Jonah, the greater Solomon, the greater Abraham and the greater Moses! He is higher than the heavens and greater than the Angels. Even the heavens aren't clean compared to Him (Job 15:15)! He is the great I AM who made everything! He has no beginning and no end! He is the Alpha and the Omega. He is THE Apostle and THE High Priest![24]

Just as Adam was put in the garden to work the ground and failed, Christ sweated great drops of blood in the garden and succeeded! He was thought to be the Gardener after His resurrection because He IS the

21. Luke 24:25-27 (New King James Version).

22. Luke 24:44 (New King James Version).

23. Hebrews 2:14-15 (New American Standard Bible).

24. Job 15:15; Matthew 28:18; Hebrews 3:1 (New King James Version).

Gardener! He is now making all things new! After He completed the work the Father had given Him to do, He cried out "It is Finished!" Then He entered into His rest and is bringing all of His posterity with Him! "For He [Christ] who has entered His rest has Himself also ceased from His works as God did from His."[25]

He has ascended into Heaven and has sat down at the right hand of the Father because the work is DONE! "Therefore He is also able to save to the uttermost those who come to God through Him, since He always lives to make intercession for them."[26] He is coming back one day to judge the living and the dead! "Now I saw heaven opened, and behold, a white horse. And He who sat on him was called Faithful and True, and in righteousness He judges and makes war. His eyes were like a flame of fire, and on His head were many crowns. He had a name written that no one knew except Himself. He was clothed with a robe dipped in blood, and His name is called The Word of God. And the armies in heaven, clothed in fine linen, white and clean, followed Him on white horses. Now out of His mouth goes a sharp sword, that with it He should strike the nations. And He Himself will rule them with a rod of iron. He Himself treads the winepress of the fierceness and wrath of Almighty God. And He has on His robe and on His thigh a name written: KING OF KINGS AND LORD OF LORDS."[27]

Look and Live

Do NOT sleep on this my friend. Refuse Him at your own peril. "See that you do not refuse Him who speaks. For if they did not escape who refused Him who spoke on earth, much more shall we not escape if we turn away from Him who speaks from heaven, whose voice then shook the earth; but now He has promised, saying, "Yet once more I shake not only the earth, but also heaven.""[28]

Look to Him and live! "Look to Me, and be saved, all you ends of the earth! For I am God, and there is no other. " Isa. 45:22[29] "Ho! Everyone who thirst, come to the waters; and you who have no money, come, buy and eat. Yes, come, buy wine and milk without money and without price."

25. Hebrews 4:10 (New King James Version).

26. Hebrews 7:25 (New King James Version).

27. Revelation 19:11-16 (New King James Version).

28. Hebrews 12:25-26 (New King James Version).

29. Isaiah 55:1 (New King James Version).

Isa. 55:1.[30] "Behold, NOW is the accepted time, behold, NOW is the day of salvation."[31] Is this fair? Not at all. This is pure grace!

"Now to Him who is able to keep you from stumbling, and to make you stand in the presence of His glory blameless with great joy, to the only God our Savior, through Jesus Christ our Lord, be glory, majesty, dominion and authority, before all time and now and forever. Amen."[32]

30. Revelation 22:17 (New King James Version).

31. 2 Corinthians 6:2 (New King James Version).

32. Jude 24-25 (New King James Version).

Hail, Thou Once Despised Jesus

Words by John Bakewell, 1757

Hail, Thou once despisèd Jesus!
Hail, Thou Galilean King!
Thou didst suffer to release us;
Thou didst free salvation bring.
Hail, Thou agonizing Savior,
Bearer of our sin and shame!
By Thy merits we find favor;
Life is given through Thy name.

Paschal Lamb, by God appointed,
All our sins on Thee were laid;
By almighty love anointed,
Thou hast full atonement made.
All Thy people are forgiven
Through the virtue of Thy blood;
Opened is the gate of heaven,
Peace is made 'twixt man and God.

Jesus, hail! Enthroned in glory,
There forever to abide;
All the heav'nly hosts adore Thee,
Seated at Thy Father's side.
There for sinners Thou art pleading,
There Thou dost our place prepare,
Ever for us interceding
Till in glory we appear.

Worship, honor, power, and blessing

Thou art worthy to receive;

Loudest praises, without ceasing,

Meet it is for us to give.

Help, ye bright angelic spirits,

Bring your sweetest, noblest lays;

Help to sing our Savior's merits,

Help to chant Immanuel's praise![33]

33. John Bakewell, "Hail, Thou Once Despised Jesus," in *A Collection of Hymns for the Use of the People Called Methodists*, ed. John Wesley (London: J. Paramore, 1780), 112–13.

Chapter 15

A Baba's Plea

"Blessed are those whose lawless deeds are forgiven, and whose sins are covered; Blessed is the man to whom the Lord shall not impute sin." Romans 4:7-8[1]

Our Greatest Need

MY DEAR CHILDREN, TULIP, London and Judah, the greatest need you will ever have is forgiveness of sins. There is nothing more important than that. You can become the most talented musician, the greatest writer, the most famous soccer player who ever lived, but if you never have your sins forgiven, you will go to hell forever. Jesus said it like this in Mark 8:36, "For what shall it profit a man, if he shall gain the whole world, and lose his own soul?"[2] My goal is to make this evident to you all in this chapter.

One of the most amazing accounts in the Gospel of Mark is with the paralytic whom Jesus healed. Mark 2:1-12 says, "When He had come back to Capernaum several days afterward, it was heard that He was at home. And many were gathered together, so that there was no longer room, not even near the door; and He was speaking the word to them. And they came, bringing to Him a paralytic, carried by four men. Being unable to get to Him because of the crowd, they removed the roof above Him; and when they had dug an opening, they let down the pallet on which

1. Romans 4:7-8 (New King James Version).
2. Mark 8:36 (New King James Version).

the paralytic was lying. And Jesus seeing their faith said to the paralytic, "Son, your sins are forgiven." But some of the scribes were sitting there and reasoning in their hearts, "Why does this man speak that way? He is blaspheming; who can forgive sins but God alone?" Immediately Jesus, aware in His spirit that they were reasoning that way within themselves, said to them, "Why are you reasoning about these things in your hearts? Which is easier, to say to the paralytic, 'Your sins are forgiven'; or to say, 'Get up, and pick up your pallet and walk'? But so that you may know that the Son of Man has authority on earth to forgive sins"—He said to the paralytic, "I say to you, get up, pick up your pallet and go home." And he got up and immediately picked up the pallet and went out in the sight of everyone, so that they were all amazed and were glorifying God, saying, "We have never seen anything like this."[3]

Do you see what just happened? This man was unable to walk. All he could do was lay in his bed all day. You and I would have looked at him and thought, "This man's greatest need is physical healing. He needs to walk." Jesus showed us that he had an even greater need. This man's greatest need, just like the rest of us, was to have his sins forgiven. He needed spiritual healing. He was "dead in his trespasses and sins."[4] He needed spiritual life. That is exactly what Jesus did for him because He loved him. The man being healed and walking was proof to all that Christ had truly forgiven his sins.

Egyptian Delight

During the 2020 Covid-19 craziness I ended up getting Covid around Thanksgiving. After having it for a couple weeks and losing my taste buds, I got a whole new appreciation for them. Eating food is not enjoyable at all when you can't taste it. I enjoy good-tasting food (my wife would object) and love to debate which food is the best. Well, for those who have had it before, know that Egyptian food is obviously the best. Don't take my word, it's biblical. Chapter and verse please? I'm glad you asked. Numbers 11:4-6 says, "Now the mixed multitude who were among them yielded to intense craving; so the children of Israel also wept again and said: 'Who will give us meat to eat? We remember the fish which we ate freely in Egypt, the cucumbers, the melons, the leeks, the onions, and the garlic; but now our whole being is dried up; there is nothing at all except this manna before our

3. Mark 2:1-12 (New King James Version).
4. Ephesians 2:1 (New King James Version).

eyes!'"[5] You see, Egyptian food is so good that the Israelites were willing to go back into slavery for it! Mic drop.

My love for culture and good food reminds me of a time when my belly led me to a great witnessing encounter. Back in Virginia Beach, there was an international food store owned by a Muslim family, where I often went for their incredible Egyptian delicacies. One summer day, I headed there to buy some groceries and get some lunch. After walking the aisles in the store and filling my shopping cart up with some basturma, olives, gebna rumi, and white cheese I got in line to check out and ordered a ta'ameya sandwich. The man who rang me up after taking my order was an American in his early 20's. As he was ringing up my groceries I struck up a conversation with him asking him how long he worked here, if he liked it, and where he was from. I asked him about his religious upbringing, what he believed about that now, how important it is or isn't to him. He had some sort of nominal Christian upbringing but was now looking into other religions. He told me about the owners of the store being Muslim. I came to find out later that the man who was cooking/making my ta'ameya sandwich in the kitchen at the time was also a Muslim.

The cashier shared some of his critiques of Christianity with me, so I asked him what he believed was required to get to heaven. He said, "That is a good question. I am not really sure."

I said, "Jesus gives us the answer in the sermon on the mount. Christ said, 'You must be perfect as your heavenly Father is perfect.' That is what's required. Perfect righteousness."[6] He looked shocked as I guess he was not expecting that answer. I explained to him how God is Holy, Righteous, Just and Good. The Bible says, "Lying lips are an abomination."[7] It says, "lust is adultery and hatred is murder."[8] I simply held up God's mirror and let him see himself in truth. I then went on to explain the consequences for sin which is Hell; eternal conscious torment.

At this point the Muslim in the kitchen who was making my sandwich had apparently been listening to our conversation. He walked out and just stood there listening as I continued sharing the Law. I explained how after we have looked in a mirror to see how filthy we really are we don't try to clean ourselves with it. We go take a shower or a bath to get

5. Numbers 11:4-6 (New King James Version).

6. Matthew 5:48 (New King James Version).

7. Proverbs 12:22 (New King James Version).

8. Isaiah 64:6 (New King James Version).

clean. I told him that is what God's Law is, a mirror. Even our "righteous deeds are filthy rags" before a holy God.[9] The Law condemns us and sends us to the One who can wash us clean. The Law is a schoolmaster that points us to Christ.[10]

I then began sharing the good news with him about Jesus Christ and Him crucified. I said, "Jesus is one-hundred-percent God and one-hundred-percent Man. He never sinned once and always did that which pleased the Father. Christ redeemed us from the curse of the Law by becoming a curse for us. He was our substitute who died in our place taking the wrath of God due to us. The Bible says, 'He made Him who knew no sin to be sin for us, so that we might become the righteousness of God in Him.'"[11] This is the gospel of Jesus Christ! It is by His work ALONE that believers are made right with God. 1 Corinthians 1:30 NASB says, "But by HIS DOING you are in Christ Jesus, who became to us wisdom from God, and RIGHTEOUSNESS..."[12] He is our righteousness! 1 Corinthians 6:11 NASB says, "Such were some of you; but you were WASHED..."[13] HE washed us! The good news of the gospel is we get CHRIST!

Answering Deedat

It was at this point that the Muslim man spoke up. He said, "Where did Jesus ever say, 'I am God, worship Me?'" Growing up with a Muslim father has its advantages at times and this was one of them. The question he asked is the famous Ahmed Deedat question. Ahmed Deedat was a very popular Muslim apologist who died in 2005. He debated many Christians throughout his life and quite frankly made them look very foolish. He was an excellent debater who would quote the Bible at will of whom my dad and many Muslims loved.

I responded by saying, "That is a great question, Mr. Deedat." I smiled and said, "I'm just kidding sir, what is your name?" After he gave me his name I said, "If I sinned against YOU, could this man (pointing to the cashier) forgive me for those sins?"

He said, "No."

9.

10. Galatians 3:24 (New King James Version).

11. 2 Corinthians 5:21 (New King James Version).

12. 1 Corinthians 1:30 (New American Standard Bible).

13. 1 Corinthians 6:11 (New American Standard Bible).

I said, "You are correct my friend. Since my sin was against you, ONLY you can forgive me for them, right?" He agreed. I then began sharing the story with him that we looked at earlier in this chapter about the paralytic. This paralytic never met Jesus and therefore never sinned against Him. Yet when the paralytic was set before Jesus, he was hoping to be healed but what happened next was infinitely greater! Jesus looked at him and said, "Son, your sins are forgiven." To prove that this man's sins had truly been forgiven Jesus looked at the paralytic and told him to "pick up your pallet and walk." And guess what? HE DID!

I said, "Here is my question for you, my Muslim friend. ALL sins are against God, correct?" He nodded in agreement. "And only God can forgive sins, right?" He nodded again. I then said, "Then what Jesus did was FAR greater than repeating those specific words that Ahmed Deedat demanded. Anyone can say they are God, but Jesus demonstrated that He is God! He forgave the sins of the paralytic because all sins are ultimately against HIM. So, in answer to your question about "Where did Jesus say, 'I am God, worship Me?'" He said that in Mark 2 when He healed the paralytic and forgave him for all his sins."

The cashier said, "Wow! That is awesome. That makes a lot of sense."

The Muslim was quiet after that. I don't think he honestly expected an answer to his question. He didn't know what to say. I pleaded with both of them to repent of their sin and trust in Christ alone. I said, "'Jesus is the way, the truth, and the life. No one comes to the Father except through Him'[14] and Acts 4:12 says, 'Nor is there salvation in any other, for there is no other name under heaven given among men by which we must be saved.'[15] Jesus is not just a sinless prophet who did miracles like Islam teaches, He is the true and living God who forgives sinners, for whom He has died."

I gave them both some Christian literature and thanked them for talking with me. I encouraged the Muslim man to read the gospel of Mark for himself instead of listening to other Muslim apologists like Ahmed Deedat or Shabir Ally. He was very respectful and said he would. I grabbed my bags of delicious Egyptian food, got my ta'ameya sandwich and headed home. I thanked God for such an awesome encounter and worshiped Him for giving me the wisdom and boldness to proclaim His gospel. This is what we are to live for Christian!

14. John 14:6 (New King James Version).
15. Acts 4:12 (New King James Version).

The Foolish Cross

I have had several conversations with people like the cashier who were raised in some sort of nominal Christian environment. It seems that almost everyone knows the Sunday school answer about how to get to heaven. "Jesus died on the cross for my sins." When I hear someone say that I will sometimes give them a scenario and ask them a question. I say, "What if a person came in here with a gun and began shooting people and I jumped in front of you to take the bullet. I died for you. Would that get you to heaven?"

They say, "No."

I then ask them to explain how Jesus Christ dying for them gets them to heaven. That is when they look at me with a confused look and say, "I don't really know."

The problem with modern evangelism of our day is we try to give people the good news BEFORE they even understand the bad news. What we need to do before we give people the gospel is give them the Law, which is a reflection of the character and nature of God. Then tell them of the consequences of breaking it; wrath of God in hell forever. They need to understand they are not good, having broken God's Law, and are now under its condemnation. That is when the gospel (For Christ also suffered for sins once for all, the righteous for the unrighteous, so that He might bring you to God)[16] will begin to make sense. Charles Spurgeon said, "The Law is the needle of the silk thread that pulls the gospel through."[17]

Another important aspect to understand about the gospel is God's righteous judgement. C.J. Mahaney said in a sermon once, "In His righteous judgment, God has determined that the just penalty for sin is death and without the shedding of blood, there is no remission of sins. Now, sin has been committed by man and therefore, only man can atone for that sin. But here's my dilemma: I can't atone for my sin. I can't. I cannot satisfy God's righteous requirements. My disobedience condemns me before a righteous God and I'm captive to sin. It is humanly impossible for me to free myself from sin. A divine rescue is necessary. I need a Savior! I need a Savior!"[18]

16. 1 Peter 3:18 (New King James Version).

17. Charles H. Spurgeon, "The Law's Failure and Fulfillment," in Metropolitan Tabernacle Pulpit (London: Passmore & Alabaster, 1889), 35:324.

18. C.J. Mahaney, "The Cross Centered Life," sermon delivered at Covenant Life Church, Gaithersburg, MD, 2002, quoted in Living the Cross Centered Life (Colorado Springs: Multnomah, 2006), 45.

This is the beauty of the gospel. Jesus is that perfect Man who atoned for our sins and the perfect God who was able to satisfy divine justice. This is why you must trust in Him, because only He can save you!

The Only Mediator

Ever been in a really bad fight with someone? I have. That is when you need a third party to mediate the situation. In this case there are two parties that are at war with one another, God and man. "Because the carnal mind is enmity against God; for it is not subject to the law of God, nor indeed can be." Romans 8:7.[19] A mediator is someone who represents BOTH parties and helps bring about reconciliation. So, in this case you need someone to represent God and someone to represent man. Here we see the brilliance of God! Jesus Christ is truly God and truly Man. He represents both parties because is He IS both parties. "For there is one God and one Mediator between God and men, the Man Christ Jesus!" 1 Timothy 2:5.[20]

Once you understand that you might still be thinking to yourself, "How can this One Man, Christ Jesus, save a multitude of men from hell by hanging on the tree for a few short hours?" Paul Washer answered this question at a Shepherds Conference in 2016. He said, "Because that One Man is worth more than all of them put together! You take mountains and molehills, crickets and clowns. You take everything, every planet, every star, every form of beauty, everything that sings, everything that brings to light and you put it all on the scale and you put Christ on the other side, and He outweighs them all! He outweighs them all."[21] Jesus Christ is of infinite value!

A Father's Heart

So, dear reader, and my precious children, this is of first importance. You are great sinners, but Christ is a greater Savior! He loves to save the worst of sinners. Is that fair? No, it is GRACE! The most glorious reality you can ever experience is to know HIM! Jeremiah 9:23-24 says, "Thus says the Lord: 'Let not the wise man glory in his wisdom, let not the mighty man

19. Romans 8:7 (New King James Version).
20. 1 Timothy 2:5 (New King James Version).
21. Paul Washer, "The Gospel of Jesus Christ," sermon delivered at Shepherds' Conference, Sun Valley, CA, March 2016, https://www.youtube.com/watch?v=8M_6rK201rM (accessed April 19, 2025).

glory in his might, nor let the rich man glory in his riches; But let him who glories glory in this, that he understands and knows Me, that I am the LORD, exercising lovingkindness, judgment, and righteousness in the earth. For in these I delight,' says the LORD."[22]

I long for the New Heavens and the New Earth where righteousness dwells! That is where God will wipe away every tear from His children's eyes. There will be no more death, nor sorrow, nor crying or pain![23] This is what every true Christian looks forward too: "People from every tribe, tongue, people and nation will be standing before the throne and before the Lamb, clothed with white robes, with palm branches in their hands, and crying out with a loud voice, saying, 'Salvation belongs to our God who sits on the throne, and to the Lamb!'" Revelation 7:9-10.[24]

Tulip, London, and Judah, never forget that those who are clothed in Christ are loved with an everlasting love. Not only are they loved by God, but NOTHING can ever separate them from that love![25]Let this hymn always remind you that the only thing you can contribute to your salvation is the sin which made it necessary, and in exchange you get Christ! Sing this hymn often and look to the Savior who washes you clean and holds you forever! Love Baba!

22. Jeremiah 9:23-24 (New King James Version).

23. Revelation 21:4 (New King James Version).

24. Revelation 7:9-10 (New King James Version).

25. Romans 8:38-39 (New King James Version).

Rock of Ages, Cleft for Me

Words by Augustus M. Toplady, 1776

Rock of Ages, cleft for me,
Let me hide myself in Thee;
Let the water and the blood,
From Thy riven side which flowed,
Be of sin the double cure,
Cleanse me from its guilt and power.

Not the labors of my hands
Can fulfill Thy law's demands;
Could my zeal no respite know,
Could my tears forever flow,
All for sin could not atone;
Thou must save, and Thou alone.

Nothing in my hand I bring,
Simply to Thy cross I cling;
Naked, come to Thee for dress;
Helpless, look to Thee for grace;
Foul, I to the fountain fly;
Wash me, Savior, or I die.

While I draw this fleeting breath,
When mine eyes shall close in death,
When I soar to worlds unknown,
See Thee on Thy judgment throne,
Rock of Ages, cleft for me,
Let me hide myself in Thee.[26]

26. Augustus M. Toplady, "Rock of Ages, Cleft for Me," in *The Gospel Magazine* (London, March 1776), 138–39.

Recommended Reading

Comfort, Ray. *God Has a Wonderful Plan For Your Life: The Myth of the Modern Message*. Bellflower, CA: Living Waters Publications, 2010.

Spurgeon, Charles Haddon, and Jeffrey Johnson. *Ten Essential Sermons of Charles Spurgeon*. Edited by Jeffrey Johnson. Conway, AR: Free Grace Press LLC, 2022.

Johnson, Jeffrey D. *The Sovereignty of God*. Conway, AR: Free Grace Press, 2023.

Spurgeon, Charles Haddon. *The Soulwinner: New Kensington, PA: Whitaker House, 2016*.

Pennington, Tom. *A Biblical Case for Cessationism: Why the Miraculous Gifts of the Spirit Have Ended*. Lincoln, NE: G3 Press, 2023.

Osman, Jim. *God Doesn't Whisper*. Sandpoint, ID: Kootenai Community Church Publishing, 2020.

Sproul, R. C. *The Holiness of God*. 2nd ed. Carol Stream, IL: Tyndale House Publishers, 2020.

Ryle, J. C. *Holiness: Its Nature, Hindrances, Difficulties, and Roots*. Peabody, MA: Hendrickson Publishers, 2007.

Bunyan, John. *The Pilgrim's Progress*. Wheaton, IL: Crossway, 2014.

Pink, Arthur W. *The Attributes of God*. Grand Rapids, MI: Baker Books, 2006.

Reisinger, Ernest C. *The Law and the Gospel*. Cape Coral, FL: Founders Press, 2019.

Washer, Paul. *The Preeminent Christ*. Grand Rapids, MI: Reformation Heritage Books, 2023.

Reeves, Stan, ed. *The 1689 Baptist Confession of Faith in modern English*. Cape Coral, FL: Founders Press, 2017.

Johnson, Jeffrey D. *The Fatal Flaw of the Theology Behind Infant Baptism*. Conway, AR: Free Grace Press, 2010.

Waldron, Sam. *The Doctrine of Last Things: An Optimistic Amillennial View*. Conway, AR: Free Grace Press, 2025.

Waldron, Sam. *A Man as Priest in his Home*. Conway, AR: Free Grace Press, 2023.

Sibbes, Richard. *The Bruised Reed and Smoking Flax*. Edinburgh: Banner of Truth Trust, 1998.

Hicks, Tom. *What is a Reformed Baptist?: An Overview of Doctrinal Distinctives*. Cape Coral, FL: Founders Press, 2025.

Bibliography

Albus, Harry J. Twentieth Century Moody: The Biography of a Man and His Mission. Chicago: Moody Press, 1962.

American Gospel: Christ Alone. Directed by Brandon Kimber. Transition Studios, 2018. Streaming.

Association of Certified Biblical Counselors. "About ACBC." Accessed April 19, 2025. https://biblicalcounseling.com/about/.

Athanasius. On the Incarnation. Translated by John Behr. Yonkers, NY: St. Vladimir's Seminary Press, 2011.

Audacity. Directed by Ray Comfort. Santa Clarita, CA: Living Waters Publications, 2015. DVD.

Augustine. Sermons on Selected Lessons of the New Testament. In A Select Library of the Nicene and Post-Nicene Fathers of the Christian Church, edited by Philip Schaff, 6:3–524. New York: Christian Literature Company, 1888.

Bakewell, John. "Hail, Thou Once Despised Jesus." In A Collection of Hymns for the Use of the People Called Methodists, edited by John Wesley, 112–13. London: J. Paramore, 1780.

Bancroft, Charitie Lees. "Before the Throne of God Above." In The Hymnal for Worship and Celebration, hymn no. 231. Waco, TX: Word Music, 1986.

The Baptist Catechism (1693). In A Faith to Confess: The Baptist Confession of Faith of 1689, 75–93. Leeds: Carey Publications, 1975.

Barnard, Shane, and Shane Everett. "Though You Slay Me." Bring Your Nothing. Fair Trade Services, 2013, compact disc.

Baucham, Voddie. "The Gospel According to Joseph." Sermon, Grace Family Baptist Church, Spring, TX, January 15, 2012. https://www.sermonaudio.com/sermoninfo.asp?SID=1151215343510.

"Benny Hinn Sith Lord (Improved Sound)." YouTube video, 2:45. Posted by "Derrick," February 25, 2008. https://www.youtube.com/watch?v=5lvU-Dislhc.

Cahill, Mark. One Thing You Can't Do in Heaven. Rockwall, TX: Biblical Discipleship Ministries, 2004.

Cahill, Mark. One Heartbeat Away: Your Journey into Eternity. Rockwall, TX: Biblical Discipleship Ministries, 2005.

Comfort, Ray. The Way of the Master. Alachua, FL: Bridge-Logos, 2006.

Comfort, Ray, and Kirk Cameron. The Way of the Master. Television program. Santa Clarita, CA: Living Waters Publications, 2003–present.

Comfort, Ray, ed. The Evidence Study Bible. Gainesville, FL: Bridge-Logos, 2011.

———, ed. The Evidence Study Bible: New King James Version. Alachua, FL: Bridge-Logos Publishers, 2011.

———. The Way of the Master. Lake Forest, CA: Living Waters Publications, 2006. Television program.

Dallimore, Arnold A. George Whitefield: The Life and Times of the Great Evangelist of the Eighteenth-Century Revival. Vol. 1. Carlisle, PA: Banner of Truth, 1970.

Duplantis, Jesse. Close Encounters of the God Kind. Metairie, LA: Jesse Duplantis Ministries, 1996. DVD.

Elliot, Elisabeth. Keep a Quiet Heart. Ann Arbor: Servant Publications, 1995.

Exit: The Appeal of Suicide. Directed by Ray Comfort. Santa Clarita, CA: Living Waters Publications, 2016. DVD.

Fireproof. Directed by Alex Kendrick. Albany, GA: Sherwood Pictures, 2008. DVD.

Friel, Todd. Don't Stub Your Toe. Fortis Institute, 2017. Gospel booklet.

Heber, Reginald. "Holy, Holy, Holy! Lord God Almighty!" In Hymns, Written and Adapted to the Weekly Church Service of the Year, no. 22. London: J. Heber, 1827.

Henry, Matthew. Commentary on the Whole Bible. Grand Rapids, MI: Zondervan, 1960.

Hinn, Benny. Good Morning, Holy Spirit. Nashville: Thomas Nelson, 1990.

It's a Wonderful Life. Directed by Frank Capra. Hollywood, CA: Liberty Films, 1946. Film.

Jillette, Penn. "A Gift of a Bible." YouTube video, 5:11. Posted by "beinzee," July 8, 2010. https://youtu.be/6md638smQd8?si=h_WiA2IcghHaxaOg

Ken, Thomas. "Doxology." In Manual of Prayers for the Use of the Scholars of Winchester College. London: n.p., 1674.

Luther, Martin. The Table Talk of Martin Luther. Edited by Thomas S. Kepler. Grand Rapids: Baker Book House, 1979.

MacArthur, John, ed. The MacArthur Study Bible. Nashville: Thomas Nelson, 1997.

———. Charismatic Chaos. Grand Rapids: Zondervan, 1992.

———. The Freedom and Power of Forgiveness. Wheaton, IL: Crossway, 1998.

Mahaney, C.J. Living the Cross Centered Life. Colorado Springs: Multnomah, 2006.

March, Daniel. "Hark, the Voice of Jesus Calling." In Hymns for the Anniversary of the Boston Young Men's Christian Association, 12–13. Boston: T.R. Marvin & Son, 1868.

Moody, Dwight L. Moody's Anecdotes and Illustrations. Chicago: Rhodes & McClure Publishing, 1898.

Morgan, Robert J., ed. The Quotable Christian. Grand Rapids: Baker Books, 1997.

Newton, John. "Amazing Grace." In Olney Hymns, no. 41. London: W. Oliver, 1779.

———. "I Asked the Lord That I Might Grow." In Olney Hymns, no. 36. London: W. Oliver, 1779.

Not Without My Daughter. Directed by Brian Gilbert. Metro-Goldwyn-Mayer, 1991. Motion picture.

Owen, John. The Mortification of Sin. 1656. Reprint, Edinburgh: Banner of Truth Trust, 2004.

Peters, Justin. "Clouds without Water." YouTube video, 2:03:45. Posted by "Justin Peters Ministries," July 15, 2014. https://www.youtube.com/watch?v=2lOnr7nmd9g.

Qur'an. Translated by Abdullah Yusuf Ali. New York: Tahrike Tarsile Qur'an, 2001.

The Qur'an. Translated by M.A.S. Abdel Haleem. Oxford: Oxford University Press, 2004.

Ravenhill, Leonard. "The Cost of Discipleship." Sermon, n.d. https://www.sermonaudio.com/sermoninfo.asp?SID=101506154150.

Sahih al-Bukhari. Translated by Muhammad Muhsin Khan. Vol. 4. Riyadh: Darussalam, 1997.

Second London Baptist Confession of Faith (1689). In A Faith to Confess: The Baptist Confession of Faith of 1689. Leeds: Carey Publications, 1975.

Spafford, Horatio G. "It Is Well with My Soul." In Sacred Songs No. 1, edited by Ira D. Sankey, Philip P. Bliss, and others, no. 42. New York: Biglow & Main, 1876.

Sproul, R.C. "The Curse Motif of the Atonement." Lecture delivered at Ligonier Ministries National Conference, Orlando, FL, 2008.

———, ed. The Reformation Study Bible. Orlando: Ligonier Ministries, 2005.

Spurgeon, Charles H "The Law and the Gospel." In The Metropolitan Tabernacle Pulpit Sermons, vol. 34, 541. London: Passmore & Alabaster, 1888.

———. "A Defense of Calvinism." In The New Park Street Pulpit Sermons, vol. 4, 337. London: Passmore & Alabaster, 1858.

———. "A Jealous God." In The New Park Street Pulpit Sermons, vol. 6, 121. London: Passmore & Alabaster, 1860.

———. "Christ's Perfection and Christ's People." In Metropolitan Tabernacle Pulpit, 36:625–636. London: Passmore & Alabaster, 1890.

———. "The Law's Failure and Fulfillment." In Metropolitan Tabernacle Pulpit, 35:317–328. London: Passmore & Alabaster, 1889.

———. "The Lesson of the Forge." In Metropolitan Tabernacle Pulpit, 28:449–460. London: Passmore & Alabaster, 1882.

———. "The Old, Old Story." In The Metropolitan Tabernacle Pulpit Sermons, vol. 10, 325. London: Passmore & Alabaster, 1864.

———. "The Restraining Prayer." In Metropolitan Tabernacle Pulpit, 25:389–400. London: Passmore & Alabaster, 1879.

———. The Soul Winner. London: Passmore & Alabaster, 1895.

Steele, Anne. "Ye Wretched, Hungry, Starving Poor." In Poems on Subjects Chiefly Devotional, vol. 1, 134–35. London: J. Buckland, 1760.

Todd Friel, Don't Stub Your Toe (Murfreesboro, TN: Fortis Institute, 2017), gospel tract.

Toplady, Augustus M. "Rock of Ages, Cleft for Me." In The Gospel Magazine, 138–39. London, March 1776.

The Valley of Vision: A Collection of Puritan Prayers and Devotions. Edited by Arthur Bennett. Carlisle, PA: Banner of Truth Trust, 1975.

Washer, Paul David. "Shocking Youth Message." Sermon, Montgomery, AL, 2002. https://www.youtube.com/watch?v=uuabITeO4ho.

———. "About HeartCry." HeartCry Missionary Society. Accessed April 19, 2025. https://heartcrymissionary.com/about/.

———. "Jacob I Loved, Esau I Hated." Sermon, Grace Community Church, Huntsville, AL, March 12, 2017. https://www.sermonaudio.com/sermoninfo.asp?SID=313171135351.

———. "The Gospel of Jesus Christ." Sermon delivered at Shepherds' Conference, Sun Valley, CA, March 2016. https://youtu.be/bkqVZm9-7jc?si=YX2gn7eIhZvJKoGR

———. "The Holiness of God." Sermon, HeartCry Missionary Conference, 2015. https://www.youtube.com/watch?v=oQol6LT2Yoo.

Watts, Isaac. "How Sweet and Awful Is the Place." In Hymns and Spiritual Songs, no. 94. London: J. Buckland, 1776.

———. "When I Survey the Wondrous Cross." In *Hymns and Spiritual Songs*, 138–40. London: J. Lawrence, 1707.

Wesley, Charles. "And Can It Be That I Should Gain." In *Hymns and Sacred Poems*, 105–7. London: Strahan, 1738.

———. "Depth of Mercy! Can There Be." In *Hymns and Sacred Poems*, 59–61. London: Strahan, 1740.

———. "Jesus, Lover of My Soul." In *Hymns and Sacred Poems*, 174–76. London: Strahan, 1740.

White, James R. What Every Christian Needs to Know About the Qur'an. Minneapolis: Bethany House, 2013.

White, James R., and Jose Ventilacion. "Debate: Who is God?" Debate, San Diego, CA, April 24, 2017. Video. https://youtu.be/YEBKNhjNxpY?si=azAAaFxAeVcz-AZH.

Whitefield, George. "The Method of Grace." In *Select Sermons of George Whitefield*, 75–76. London: Banner of Truth Trust, 1958.

Wurmbrand, Richard. *Tortured for Christ*. Bartlesville, OK: Living Sacrifice Book Company, 1967.

Zwayne, Julia, and Ray Comfort. *Audacity: Love Can't Stay Silent*. Alachua, FL: Bridge-Logos, 2016.

www.ingramcontent.com/pod-product-compliance
Lightning Source LLC
Chambersburg PA
CBHW071443090426
42737CB00011B/1760